DESTINATION TURN UP

A NOT-SO-NORMAL LIFE

EZEKIEL SMITH

WESTBOW
PRESS®
A DIVISION OF THOMAS NELSON
& ZONDERVAN

WestBow Press books may be ordered through booksellers or by contacting:

WestBow Press
A Division of Thomas Nelson & Zondervan
1663 Liberty Drive
Bloomington, IN 47403
www.westbowpress.com
844-714-3454

ISBN: 978-1-9736-1864-5 (sc)
ISBN: 978-1-9736-1863-8 (e)

Library of Congress Control Number: 2018901842

Print information available on the last page.

WestBow Press rev. date: 05/16/2022

CONTENTS

Acknowledgments xi

Introduction xiii

1 Let's Go to Hawaii... 1
2 Here We Go.. 17
3 The Boy.. 35
4 Why Suicide? 45
5 The Ten Trials of Troy, One-Four 69
6 Ten Trials of Troy, Five-Ten... 79
7 The Story of a Ph.D. – Prayer,
   Hard Work, and Dedication 99
8 Blessed is the Man Who Finds
   a Wife – The Love Story... 107
9 Season of Love and Love that Lasts!................................117
10 The Importance of Community and Family.................... 127
11 The Privilege of Prison,
   the Story of Mario; and that Day 133
12 Destination Anywhere 151
13 The FSS and The Sewer...169

Epilogue 185

About the Author... 187

Warning: Peculiar Days Ahead

ACKNOWLEDGMENTS

First and foremost, I would like to thank my lovely wife, Stacy, for supporting me, encouraging me, and laughing with me through this whole ordeal. Next, I would like to thank my daughter who let her daddy type when she desperately wanted to go on a daddy/daughter date to the beach. Also, I would like to thank my Dad for loving me all these years through all these wild adventures. I'm so thankful for having a family that supported me when I wanted to throw in the towel on the book. Huge thanks to all those, and you know who you are, who shared your stories with me and confided in me over the years. Thanks to all my awesome editors for the editing, the invaluable feedback, and help through this whole fiasco. Last, but not least, thank You, God, for letting me live through all these experiences.

INTRODUCTION

Wow, have you ever ended up in a place where you never imagined you would be? On a drive to work one morning, I met a guy named Don. He was telling me how he liked to park in front of this old church with a cross out in front of it. Then he started to share about his life now and how it had completely changed. I asked, "How so?" He turned off his truck and started to explain.

For some, showing up to work seems just like another typical day, but hopefully today will be different. Some offices are not the ones that we ever expected or asked for, and mine just so happens to be the world. As a business owner, each day can certainly vary. On the morning in question, parking in a different space didn't seem like much of a change. However, as the day unfolded it was certainly where I needed to be. Each of us can meet with people anywhere, at any moment, if we are willing to step out of our comfort zone or our vehicle as in this case. So, that's when it happened. The man who started talking to me said, "That's funny, my office is across the street from yours. Usually every morning I just pull up in front of this cross here and pray for my day and for the people who work here."

I thought to myself, "I often wonder who is up at such early hours praying and seeking God." This man and his journey were used by God to encourage people like you and me, reminding us that we are not alone in life or when we are praying. This certainly encouraged me, starting my day knowing that people like him are praying for me.

So why have faith?
This is a great question for anyone thinking
about the purpose of their life.
For me it is evaluating what is next and
how to serve and help people.

The day was like any other day. I woke up and just started praying to the Lord, hoping that He would guide each step of my day. The book I had been reading said that God will do just that. He will ordain the steps of a righteous man. He will give us hope when we have none. We can all step out of our daily routine every now and then to give a true testimony of our lives and walks with Christ. Each day is an opportunity to share our faith. It is all about Faith and living it out. Faith to each person is something that they hold closely. For Christians, it means being a disciple, one who trusts and follows Christ Jesus. In my own life, it meant trusting when God moved and put it on my heart to just start writing this book. Hopefully each of you will be encouraged in your relationship with God or will discover Who He truly is. Well, now the stage is set for the way.

What follows are the Godly-inspired stories from my own life, the lives of people around me, and the ways they each unfold before us. First, I would like to thank you for not closing this book, and I pray that the testimonies in this book will encourage you and impact your life the same way many other people's testimonies and lives have impacted mine. Our stories matter, and God gives these stories to us to share and draw others close to God.

It would be nice if everyone could write the account of their lives. We have glimpses of other people's lives through modern technology of what people would like us to see; however, we do not have the full picture. You, too, have a story when life unfolds, and it certainly will! Your own journey has led you to the point of reading this book at this very moment. I pray that these stories will give you new insight on how God can use you to share His amazing love, forgiveness, and grace with people all around you.

What are you currently learning in life? Maybe it is to teach others about forgiveness. Maybe it is learning about the meaning of fellowship. Maybe it is about learning to trust God. Better yet – maybe it is knowing that you are never alone!

> For He has said, "I will never leave you nor
> forsake you." Hebrews 13:5b (ESV)

Note: In this book some of the names and places have been changed to protect the awesome individuals who have shared their stories with me and now with you.

CHAPTER ONE

Let's Go to Hawaii

If you see a wave, go surf it. What good are waves when you can't surf them? On the island, it was an amazing experience to surf some of the largest waves in the world. One sunny afternoon on the North Shore of Hawaii a solid north-northwest swell was hitting the island, and my goal was to surf these massive waves. I knew deep down that this could be my last day alive if I paddled out and entered the 20+foot surf. My friends on the island were just calling it 10 to 12 Hawaiian. The North Shore boys are always underscoring the surf size. If it's 30 feet on the face of the wave some only call it 15 feet. The size is measured by the back of the wave in this case. When a person paddles out into surf like that, I hope they know they are in God's hands. At any moment, if you go down and take a bad wipeout, you could die.

Note for any of you thinking of surfing big waves: if you are ever in doubt please do not go out in the lineup! If Phantoms (a heavy outer reef break) is breaking on the outside, it is a clear indicator that the surf is very big. The life guards have their hands full on days like these and would say don't go in or even near the water. Some would call it survival surfing! Hopefully you know where you are going if you do decide to paddle out. There are only two places, heaven or being eternally separated from God, otherwise known as hell.

On this particular day, when I paddled out, not only was

the surf potentially life threatening but after paddling out to the line-up I made a rookie mistake and took off on the second wave of the set. Bad idea because there are usually two more of the same size waves behind it. Unfortunately, on the takeoff I dug a rail and knew I was in for a long beat-down. I wiped out so hard. I remember skipping down the face of the wave. I got sucked over the falls then pushed down under the water until my ears started hurting really bad, and I knew this could be my last seconds. I gasped for air as I came up out of the water. I was choking on the sea foam above the ocean. Some call this the foam layer. It was about a foot of foam on the surface and things were not looking good at this point. After climbing the ladder (which means pulling yourself up to the surface by climbing up your surfboard leash) I knew things went from bad to worse. This is when I prayed and told God, "If I live through this, I have to live for the right purpose. God, I will live for you." I took another set wave on top of the head, and was dragged down even deeper. When your ears start to hurt, you know you're pretty far down. Unless you are a fish and can breathe under water, this is not where you want to be. For me, personally, I was pretty deep in sin and needed to be rescued. I needed to be rescued both spiritually and physically in this disastrous situation. God was the only One who could help me with each one. He came through on this day, like He always does, by His grace! I had now committed myself to Him and from then on, my walk would be His walk. Some people may say that surfing brings them the most fulfilment in the world, and after giving my life to God, I realize that living my life for Jesus Christ means more than any size wave I've ever ridden.

But I do not account my life of any value nor as precious
to myself, if only I may finish my course and the ministry
that I received from the Lord Jesus, to testify to the
gospel of the grace of God. Acts 20:24 (NIV)

Let's rewind for a moment and see how I even got myself there in the first place. I'll hopefully never forget the day. I was at VT, (Virginia Polytechnic and State University) also known as Virginia Tech, staring at a computer screen and wondering where my next steps in life would go. This was after finishing a Master's degree and then pursuing my Ph.D. that was in EDCI, healing up from a serious eye injury, and the two surgeries that were needed to put my eye back together. Needless to say – God got my attention with almost losing my right eye, and I was reminded of Paul in the Bible. I remember someone telling me that this guy, Paul, was blind. While staring at the computer screen, I decided to buy a one-way ticket to an island in the middle of the Pacific Ocean, called Oahu. What was I thinking? I wasn't, but I just had faith, as in trust, that God had a plan for me there. While this would ordinarily be considered a rash or even reckless decision, God had put it on my heart, and I was at peace with the decision. It was about trusting God. This was confirmed when I asked a friend of mine, Ike, if he would join me for this next adventure. Little did I know the impact this trip would have on his life or on mine.

After being on the island for about two weeks, I remember looking up at a massive glass building, the Waikiki Landmark towers. It was then that I noticed a guy who was like anyone we meet, a stranger at first, but someone who would become a friend.

His name was John. It was kind of funny: on the bottom of his surfboard he had spray painted John 3:16. I thought to myself, "Is this guy for real? Either he is a Christian or he is just being outright ridiculous. I mean who puts that, in big bold print, on their surfboard?" So often we see people associate themselves with Scripture but don't see a commitment to the Lord. This guy, John, was in fact, committed. As we were talking, he mentioned he was heading to a local surf shop on the island. It just so happened I was going to the same surf shop.

At the surf shop, he started talking and laughing with one of the workers named Caleb, who seemed to know who he was. As I listened to their conversation it was clear to me that John really loved God. Before he left the store, I asked if he had a minute. His response was, "Yeah, sure," like any surfer I know. After telling him my story of buying a one-way ticket and looking for a place to live, he smiled and said, "Hop in my car." I asked, "Well, where would we be heading?" In a nutshell, he said, "I'm on the way to Bible study, would you care to join me?" My response was some sort of a reluctant yes.

Maybe I forgot to mention that this day was the last day I could stay in my current living situation, and I did not want to be without a place to live, even in Hawaii. I initially lived with a newlywed couple, and I had Ike with me. John said he needed to stop by his current house. I went with John to his house and met a gentleman by the name of Chris. I came to find out he was another Christian, and Chris challenged me on several separate occasions about my own personal commitment to Christ. His first challenge to me was living out my walk with God. That was when John chimed in and said, "Hey Troy, that room over there used to belong to our other roommate, and now that's where you'll be living." I smiled and laughed, praising God for showing up at that moment to provide me a home. I thought to myself, "What an amazing God we serve."

Wow! Almost 5000 miles away from VT and God had provided a place for me to stay during this season of my life, and I got to know the Lord and see His faithfulness in the life He had given me.

"Therefore, I tell you, do not be anxious about your life, what you will eat or what you will drink, nor about your body, what you will put on. Is not life more than food, and the body more than clothing? Look at the birds of the air: they neither sow nor reap nor gather into barns, and yet your heavenly Father feeds them. Are you not of more value than they? And which of you by being anxious can add a single hour to his span of life?" Matthew 6:25-27(ESV)

While in Hawaii, I learned many things about God's character and His patience with us. When God takes us out of our comfort zone, He meets us right where we are. Hawaii would be the place where I would learn what it means to honor, love, and respect both women and myself. It's funny when God calls us to a place. It's in that place where He usually shows us what we need to change in our personal lives. When you think of Hawaii, you think of beautiful, tan people in great physical shape. I was surrounded by beautiful women. This is exactly where God called me to purity in my personal life. "God, really?" He certainly does have a sense of humor. It had never been easier, especially playing football at the college level, to find women to date. It only seemed natural to get involved in relationships with women like I always had, when the whole time God was asking me to be in an intimate relationship with Him. He wanted my heart, my desires, my dreams, and my hopes. He wants yours too.

He's not just calling some of us to purity, but all of us. Thinking to myself, "Lord not me." There's something to be said for men who honor women with their eyes and protect them, not preying on them or hurting them. Furthermore, there is also something to be said for women who respect men, their boundaries, and their weaknesses. Many nights I've asked God for forgiveness for the way I have dishonored Him in my life. Before a person can think about leading others, he must first be led by God's Spirit, be surrendered, and be obedient to God. Nothing is impossible with God, but living for Him and His glory certainly does not come naturally. Surrendering our desire is not something that ever comes easily! It only happens in the supernatural, so here is my explanation of it.

Before I was in that computer lab booking my ticket to Hawaii, I recall asking my dad if he was a Christian. It was an awkward conversation and felt very uncomfortable, yet I knew deep down that this would be one of the most important conversations I would ever have with my dad. When the Lord places something on your heart, it is for a reason. Later, I would come to find out that was the moment my dad had given his life to Christ. After looking back at one of my journal entries, the date was April 14, 2004. That Wednesday night would be a night I hopefully will always remember! What an honor and blessing it is to know that God has a plan, and we can be part of that plan when we're willing to act in obedience.

Little did I know that same trip would be the one where my friend, Ike, would also deepen his own personal walk with God. Yet at the time if you would have asked him, he was so angry with me. He even admitted how he felt like God seemed to provide more for me than him. And yes, I can say that I believe God provides for everyone, sometimes at different times and in different ways than we would expect. The complexity of God's character could never be summed up in a book. God's ways are mysterious. God's intricate plan to use a trip to an island would end up being the pathway for both Ike and me to come to know the Lord in a more intimate way.

What does it mean to live out our walk for Christ? For me, writing this book is what really living for Him looks like, because I did not want to write this book. However, when He put it on my heart and others confirmed it, I was obedient. Many people have continued to encourage me to continue to write it. Our walk with Him is the reason God gives us life, and I believe that. He spared my life on the North Shore that day when I could have died surfing. His loving grace for me is the reason I now have this chance to write these words to you. The Lord called me to surrender that day. You might ask yourself what this means.

It means thanking God for the life He has given you and loving Him enough to be obedient and submit to His plan for your life. My life is not just for myself but to show others the love of Christ. It is all about love. Aloha Ke Akua, and Iesu Ke Aloha! This means God is love, and Jesus is love. Share this with others!

One cannot show love until they, themselves, have first been shown love. Someone shared this with me while living in Hawaii the first time. God loved us first. As my life was spared that day,

I knew that God was calling me to do the right thing. The right thing was to really dedicate my life to Him by trusting in Him and ultimately living for Him, not just saying I would live for Him and denying Him with my actions. This would turn out to be His perfect will for my life. Hopefully as you read this you stop and take a moment. If you can relate to any of these stories, this one or the ones to come, realize that God has a plan and a purpose for you.

"For I know the plans I have for you," declares the LORD, "plans to prosper you and not to harm you, plans to give you hope and a future." Jeremiah 29:11. NIV

If you desire to live out your walk with Christ and to dedicate yourself to Him, pray this simple prayer:

Lord, today, at this moment, I am surrendering my life to You. Lord, have Your will and way in this life You have given me. God, I know that Your plan for my life is better than anything I could ever imagine. Today forgive me of my sin. I accept that Jesus already paid for my sins on the cross when He died and rose again, and from this point forward have Your way in me. May Your will be done in my life here on earth as it is in Heaven. In Jesus' name I pray, amen.

If you prayed this prayer, your life can and will be satisfying and meaningful. That doesn't mean it will always be easy. My prayer is that your motivation now is to help and serve others not for your reward, but for God's glory. If you know any Christians, they would love to know about your decision and could probably help you find a Bible-believing church. I always said: "If life gets any better, I would be dead." Because when I pass away, by the grace of God, I will be in Heaven. I can rest in that hope every day, and people hopefully see the peace in my heart. We just need to have faith and believe. It seems so easy to say these things, but my friends would always tell me, "Don't pray to die." I would say in return, "My prayer is to die to my flesh." When we walk by faith and not by sight, it is a wild ride. Our minds can easily drift away from what is really important due to all the distractions and preoccupations, just as a child's does when he first enters an amusement park. It is sort of clouded by all the things in modern life, instead of what is really important, which is loving God and spending time with friends and family.

In the movie, *The Chronicles of Narnia*, this idea was illustrated by the children's lives unfolding before the Creator as they walk into an unknown world, Narnia, beyond the closet door. Just like in the movie, we may never know what is behind the door unless we are willing to open it. Hopefully people are willing to open the doors to their hearts to let Christ come in. That's exactly what was happening when I gave my life to the Lord.

Ask, and it will be given to you; seek, and you will find; knock and it will be opened to you. Matthew 7:7(ESV)

Back during Christmastime in December 1988, I remember my friend, Ann, and her mom, Linda, asking me if I knew what it was like to have a personal relationship with Christ. I wasn't even sure who Christ was. Who is Jesus anyway? I remember asking a lot of questions, but I also trusted they would share the truth with me. They did. I remember being in front of an empty fireplace, remembering that there was no fire inside. But on this chilly winter day, after praying and accepting Jesus Christ into my heart, I knew I was saved and this gave me peace no matter what I had previously gone through in life or what situations laid ahead.

I remember sort of trying to explain to my dad, "I'm saved now. I gave my life to Jesus." He said, "That's great son." I'm not even sure that he knew what had taken place. But it didn't matter. I knew God knew this was my new life, and I am a new creation! It was as if I had a new hard drive. I had a completely fresh start. When God comes into our life He makes all things new. It is a new operating system. We now operate and move in God's love, and we are restored. Occasionally we can all have a crash or glitch every now and then, but we are still new. When we give our life to God He renews us, restores us, and redeems us. Think about an old rusty 1977 classic car on the side of the road. God takes us in and completely restores us! He straightens out our frame, gives us a new engine, and new paint job.

Later in life, during my college years, I found myself in an X-Ray room at Schiffer Health Center at VT. The day I gave my life to Jesus there was a fireplace in the room, but no fire in it. That day at Schiffer Health Center, God put that fire in my heart for Him. I remember it clearly. I paused and there was a shift, almost God gave me a deeper understanding and insight. I learned to daily ask Christ to fill me with His Spirit on April 27, 2002. I don't know how to explain it except it was as if my eyes and ears were really opening to seeing what God had for me, and He made things even clearer for me, in prayer by really listening to Him. Another prayer I prayed was for brokenness, humility, and patience. This was a suggestion from two of my Virginia Tech teammates. One of them was the QB that backed up a future NFL superstar quarterback, and he also backed me up with prayer and encouragement. I really do miss this person. His name was Cole Sanders, he often reminded me to not ever take for granted when God puts someone in your life for a brief time. I'm sure some of you are even thinking now of people who have made great impacts in your life. This prayer of brokenness, humility, and patience would then lead me to understand the ten trials of Troy, which we will get to later. I asked God to fill me with His Spirit and teach me what brokenness, humility, and patience looked like. *Warning: do not pray this prayer unless you are willing to go through a lot of hardship and suffering.*

The Bible, God's Word, talks about suffering. It does not talk about *if* we will suffer, but *when* we suffer. Even when we go to church, we may suffer due to people's sinful nature. No one wants to be in a church that judges them or ridicules them. They want to be in a place of fellowship that helps to encourage them while seeing God transform their lives. Church can be messy, because we are all imperfect people. God calls us to love one another despite what we have done to hurt one another. Part of surrendering to God means giving up your will or even wanting to be right, correct, or seeing it from only your own perspective. This is forgiveness and giving others a little bit of the immeasurable grace God has given us.

If we surrender to His will, God gives our life meaning and purpose. When we go to God, He provides us with answers and strength. In Romans 7:25 (NLT), we read that He is the answer to a broken, hurting world. God grants us wisdom and courage when we need it most. With God, all things are possible, and He provides us with all we really need in this life. He surrounds us with people who will help us; He encourages us; and He give us wisdom. When we pray, we discover the many wonders of God and His Word. When we seek the Lord, God provides us with the ability to love our family, friends, and community – all because of God's love for them and our faith in Him. John Piper calls this Christian hedonism and defines it as, *"God is most glorified in us when we are most satisfied in him."*[1] The Bible really is all about God's redeeming love.

God has a plan for our lives. Here is an example of His plan in my life when I was willing to trust Him. What a blessing that God would bring this incredible woman, Stacy, to me, who became my loving wife. What an amazing example of God's love she is to me, our family, and others. Where do I begin in describing all the wonderful characteristics of God that she exemplifies? A wife like Stacy expresses her utmost patience and gives warm smiles to help me along this journey of faith. She's a strong woman. The day I met the love of my life, was one of those hard days when you just want to go home and relax. A close friend named Tom called me to ask if I wanted to go to a social event with people from his church. I was very reluctant but thought, "What do I have to lose?" I could have lost out on an amazing woman that God had ordained for me by following my own will instead of trusting in His will. Once I was there, I remember seeing a young lady with blonde hair, blue eyes, and a beautiful smile. Not knowing that this was my future wife, I did what I always do and tried to set her up with the guy who invited me there. For some reason, I always tried to set up

---

[1] Piper, J. (2011). *Desiring God.* Colorado Springs, Colo.: Multnomah.

every girl with one of my friends. This was just par for the course, avoiding commitment.

After seeing her again later at an outdoor bonfire at a different venue with some other friends, that I didn't know until later was a singles event, a man asked me if I was interested in anyone there. I said at this point I was in the bachelor-for-life club. Why not?

When I look back I remember reading a Bible verse that says, "Could you bring me some water and some for my camels as well?" One day, Stacy asked me if I wanted some water, and I said yes and asked for water for my camels too. She brought back water for me and my two friends, Tom and Bill. Yes, those two guys love me enough to let me refer to them as camels, funny but true. This is when I knew that Stacy was the one for me. She has such a servant's heart and it encourages me to do the same. "Blessed is the man who finds a wife." I know that it was God who found my wife, and He placed her in front of me. God knows what He is doing, and for those of you reading this book who have a desire to be married, please know that your first love is Christ. He is faithful to meet all your needs according to His will. If a guy like me was able to get married, then there is hope for everyone. Guaranteed.

> Then he prayed, "Lord, God of my master Abraham, make me successful today, and show kindness to my master Abraham. See, I am standing beside this spring, and the daughters of the townspeople are coming out to draw water. May it be that when I say to a young woman, 'Please let down your jar that I may have a drink,' and she says, 'Drink, and I'll water your camels too'—let her be the one you have chosen for your servant Isaac. By this I will know that you have shown kindness to my master." Genesis 24:12-14 (NIV)

CHAPTER TWO

Here We Go

This chapter is dedicated to the most amazing person in my life, Jesus. He is very real to me, and I pray that He will become just as real to you. I have learned over the years, like many other everyday people, pastors, teachers, and evangelists, the need to make time for the Lord. Every relationship takes time to build, and your relationship with God is no different. The hard part for many people, however, is setting aside time to wait for Him and listen to what He puts on your heart. As the years have gone by, I have learned to enjoy the blessings of ministry and surrendering my will to His. Equally important, however, I have learned to enjoy being in God's presence, knowing that He loves me and His Holy Spirit leads me.

We are often called to listen to God. This means spending time in prayer. When we make plans that do not center around God, we need to be prepared for God to change them. Some of my favorite questions that I have learned to ask myself:

- What has God been teaching me?
- How will I live differently by what He has shown me?
- Have I been faithful to the Lord? Marriage? Family? Ministry?
- Do I enjoy life?

When asking myself this list of questions, I have come to realize that God can speak to our hearts if we are ready to hear from Him and listen. During these still, quiet, moments in life, the Lord inspires us to write things down. Hope and believe to see those things you write down come to fruition. Some people love goal-planning sessions. I like to call goals "amazing moments we live for." When we live for the Lord, then our goals and desires line up with His. He guides us to what He has called us to do next. He sometimes doesn't give us all the clarity, but He calls us to trust in Him, love Him, and listen to Him.

We are so often caught up in doing the things of normal life that we forget how to just be. We forget how to be in love with the Lord and spend time with Him. We are called to love God and love people, which starts with commitment to and a relationship with Christ. There are five things in which we all could benefit from being intentional in:

1. Loving people
2. Caring for them
3. Listening to them
4. Praying for their needs
5. Encouraging them by communicating God's love for them.

Since our friendship with God was restored by the death of his Son while we were still his enemies, we will certainly be saved through the life of his Son. So now we can rejoice in our wonderful new relationship with God because our Lord Jesus Christ has made us friends of God. Romans 5:10-11(ESV)

As believers, we are called to nurture our relationship with God. Organically, from that relationship, we develop a desire to spread the Good News of God's grace that came to us through Jesus, to allow His Holy Spirit to lead us, and to love one another. I've heard the term "accessible grace," and after reading about God's grace, let's reflect and respond by recognizing the wonderful, abundant grace He has made available to every one of us. One thing the Lord has taught me over the years is that Faith is a journey. When we get out of the way, He can make a path for us. In my own life, this past year has been sort of a roller coaster, some ups and downs, but by His grace, a lot more ups!

Hopefully this book gives you an opportunity to see that our God is a redeeming God. The whole story of the Bible is about Jesus Christ and His power of redemption, reconciliation, and restoration for the life He has given you.

"Apart from God, we can do nothing." John 15:5b (NLT)

When we trust God with our lives, we believe that God will provide for our needs. Many of us do not know where we may be heading next, but God does! He is preparing you. It starts in our hearts, but be willing to make plans, bringing them before God before you take the next step. A devoted person who loves God's Word and His people can do amazing things with Him leading. I have learned over the years that we are not to doubt our righteousness in Christ.

"And when he comes, he will convict the world concerning sin and righteousness and judgment: concerning sin, because they do not believe in me; concerning righteousness, because I go to the Father, and you will see me no longer; concerning judgment, because the ruler of this world is judged." John 16:8-11(ESV)

In context, we must remember that Satan, too, has been judged. The Holy Spirit, therefore, convicts us to live a righteous life. Satan condemns and makes people feel guilty – guilt does not come from God. When true conviction takes place, it leads a person to repentance. Repentance means making a U-turn, turning away from sin, because God's love is greater than sin. God's kindness leads us to repentance! (Romans 2:4) We, as Christians, are made righteous in Christ. We are loved by God. Your sin is forgiven because of what Christ has done. It is not about earning God's approval or anyone else's for that matter. Christ takes away all sin, not just some of it. When we focus on sin and not on God, it leads us off track. God's kindness and love leads us to a place of restoration and forgiveness. Observe what the Word says; apply what you read to your life; pray about where God is leading you; and look back at how God has answered your prayers.

- Observe what The Word says.
- Apply what you read in the Word to your life.
- Pray about where God is leading you.
- Look back at how God has answered your prayers.

God's Provision

This is a story of two large checks. When we are serving the Lord, God has a way of showing us how He can provide for our future. Here's the story of Stephen, who walked to the back of a church property and saw a shed. He heard movement in the shed and was not sure of what was taking place, or if a large animal of some kind was in there. Inside, he discovered a person who had no place to stay for the night. It was a cold December day and the thought of a person staying out in the cold all night moved Stephen to compassion. Sometimes compassion means listening to a person first and then honoring them when they desire to be left alone. However, that does not mean that you do not have to ask if there is a way that you could help them in any other way. Think about being in the cold, sometimes a warm meal or a heavy coat or blanket could be a simple way to bless another person. About five years later, that same homeless person that he helped, sent him a very large sum of money after the sale of their family's estate in California. Sometimes we are not sure of how God may provide, but when we are kind enough to help those who have nothing to give in return, it shows our heart and His. Those are life-changing experiences that we may not have been aware of in the moment. The Lord seems to move at a moment's notice, year after year.

The future for some of us may seem very bleak. God, however, has a plan. Over the years, it has become clearer to me that God may indeed be redirecting our lives. We're witnessing Him opening doors that we once thought were closed. As we continue to serve the Lord and devote ourselves to living for Him, we see He can do the impossible. Just in the last year, a ministry that we have partnered with for many years had some surprising donations. We know that God uses the small donations just as much as the large to provide for His glory.

It makes me smile knowing that God can provide financially

at just the right time in a person's life. Looking back, we can and have seen where God meets specific needs for people who have had financial struggles. While money all too often becomes the source of idolatry, He uses money as a tool. Ultimately what the world needs now is the Good News of the Gospel, which money cannot buy. We cannot earn or buy God's favor in any way, shape, or form. You can trust in Jesus, even if you cannot trust in anyone or anything else. God is calling us to be people of integrity, and He does not force things to happen.

Another memory in my personal life was surviving three different car accidents in which I should have died. When I think about how fragile life is, it reminds me of God's faithful hand at work in our personal lives. It's all about Jesus! Have you ever seen the bumper sticker that says, "God is my co-pilot?" Give Him the driver's seat!

A friend of mine once told me: "It's better to start out with nothing and have a lot later in life than to have a lot at the beginning and have nothing at the end of your life." When I heard this statement, I thought to myself, "That is very true." I believe the same principle applies to our journey here on Earth. It's better to come into the world not having anything and leaving with our Lord and Savior Jesus Christ, meeting him safely in heaven where there will be a place of comfort for eternity than leaving with nothing – without Him.

Donald is a sanitation disposal worker. One day a trash truck rolled over Him, crushing his arm and leg. He was going to die, or so we thought. Little did I know that one day I would run into this man again with my wife, only to learn of the hardship that he had experienced in his life. Donald lost his wife. After two epileptic seizures and a car accident during the second seizure, she ended up passing. My thoughts were, "How could anyone go through this and still be so thankful?" His response was, "Without Jesus, I couldn't be." Wow, what an encouragement to me. When I find myself thinking life seems difficult, I remember Donald.

One night, a young man I knew was driving home like he had done many nights before, but this night would be his last. Unfortunately, this young man's vehicle rolled over, killing him. This would be the hardest thing for his dad to hear. This dad, however, knew the Lord and that is what carried him through the loss and emotional pain. A pain which most of us could never imagine – having a child and then losing them. Similarly, another father was a pastor, and he found out that his son was shot one evening. When I think of parents who have lost their children it reminds me of how fragile not only our lives are but also people close to us ... We need to be thankful for the moments we have with our loved ones.

> Job arose and tore his robe and shaved his head and fell
> on the ground and worshiped. And he said, "Naked I
> came from my mother's womb, and naked shall I return.
> The Lord gave, and the Lord has taken away; blessed
> be the name of the Lord." In all this Job did not sin
> or charge God with wrong. Job: 1:20-22 (ESV)

Another brief illustration: a man was stranded on an island, and he called out to God saying, "God, could you please rescue me!" He went to go gather some more things that he could salvage from the wreck and use on the island so that he could live. But when he returned, somehow the fire that he had started spread and burnt all the things that he had previously collected. He cried out to God saying, "Why would you do this, God? I have nothing, yet you took everything from me, and I have no one here. I'm completely isolated and alone." Little did he know, that a rescue boat would come ashore and rescue him. He asked the people rescuing him, "How did you know that I was stranded on this island in the middle of nowhere?" Their response: "We realized that you had made a fire, and we could see your smoke signal from really far away." The reason I share this story and these others with you is that when you feel like everything is going wrong, and you are in pain or seem to be abandoned, God knows exactly what He's doing. He has a plan, even in our adversities.

If the Gospel has not changed your life, have you really heard the Gospel? But, if you have heard the Gospel, and it has not changed your life, what makes you think it will change others, unless they see you living out your faith?! Today, this very moment, God can change you if you put your hope, faith, and trust in Jesus Christ.

The Airplane Theory

Romans 8:2, Christ has set us free.

Romans 12:2, we have hope that He can change us.

Sin is like gravity on an airplane. Sin weighs us down. Sin does not go away. When we have the Holy Spirit rocket ship, He gives us the power to take off and continue fighting the gravity of sin. God, in Christ, has offered us the chance to always begin anew. Gravity doesn't stop a rocket ship, nor does sin stop the

Holy Spirit from empowering a person who believes and repents. Fellow believers can help us to remember this important truth when some of our circumstances and mistakes have blinded us. Every day is a new day, but sometimes growing up or maturing as a Christian can be very slow and painful. Remember, it is a process. Sometimes you will see a Christian act in a superficial way. At these moments, we are called to give them grace. God uses a process in our lives. Through a hardship, He can produce peace, patience, and hope. This is done in our lives by the Holy Spirit. Even in our times of difficulty, life is like our classroom. Trouble is much like our exam, and the Holy Spirit is our teacher through the entire process. You can see by these analogies that the Holy Spirit is multi-faceted, and He gives us the power to defeat sin when temptation comes.

The following is a story of Joanne, who God put in our lives to understand the brokenness that young people can face today. As early as she could remember, her parents always fought. They were drug users, sellers, and growers of marijuana. She grew up, and they had no stove in their home. They had to use a plug-in burner, and at times they had no electricity, which also meant no hot water. The sad part was she didn't know it. She thought, "Our mom was so great, letting us shower in the rain." Joanne's mom moved from man to man and always fought with them. Then, at an early age, Joanne began to go to the church across the street from her home. She had always heard a voice telling her everything would be okay. When she was with the people at the church fellowship, she learned that the voice she heard was the voice of God, her Savior. One night, when she was four years old, she hid in her bedroom closet with her two-year-old brother, while her father beat her mother with a broom. After the ambulance took them all away, Joanne and her family were displaced, separated through dysfunction and the legal system.

A few years later, Joanne's mom dropped them off at a gas station in Tennessee, and a man came and told them that he was their dad. He did look kind of familiar to her young eyes, so they went with him thinking it would be okay. She was only eight, and her brother was six. They were two of three white children in an elementary school, and they had to learn to fight very fast, because they were picked on for being white in a predominantly black area. Their dad lived with another woman and her baby. The parents worked a lot, and they hated the kids. They often locked them outside. They would let them in to do chores and sleep, but that was about it. Later, Joanne ended up becoming a young, single mother, because of her irresponsibility and the lack of a father in her life.

There was a bus that would come into the area, and they would jump on the bus which took them to a little church down the road. She would get on, and every Sunday there was safety there. This little church didn't care about parental consent. When she came home she would often get beaten with a willow tree switch until she bled, because she went to church. She told herself that this was normal. Yet, Joanne knew that everything would be okay, because the Voice said it would be okay.

One day, however, Joanne came home from school, and discovered that all her clothes were in trash bags. She and her brother were locked out – it was February, and it was very cold. Joanne and her brother prayed that their dad would come back and that he would help them. He did show up, and he took them to a little hotel. She never really asked her father any questions. Later the next day she would end up traveling 500 miles away in the back of a little covered truck. She didn't know why she was going that far, but her dad had started dating an 18-year-old woman who would eventually become their stepmom. Sadly, she had no church to go to in this area, but she could hear the voice of God telling her to read the Bible. The hardest part of this new arrangement was that her stepmom's dad ended up moving in with them, and he became physically, verbally, and sexually abusive.

Her mom found out about the abuse, and she gave Joanne to a person who said she was her sister. Joanne was only twelve at the time and was very confused. By the time she was in 5ᵗʰ grade she had attended over twenty different schools. She really enjoyed school, and the adults were usually nice to her, but her mom still moved from man to man and place to place. Basically, she was homeless and would just sleep wherever they could. Joanne ended up eventually becoming a part of the foster care system, then later in life she would be given to her aunt.

At thirteen Joanne's parents wanted her back, but she did not want to go back to the abuse. It was awful, so she ended up running away. She would stay with people who would let her baby-sit for them. She was a hostess at a restaurant for a time. She managed to stay in school and get good grades and eventually she lived in a homeless shelter for teenagers. Being in and out of foster care was tough. Then one day a woman, that she still calls mom today, who was a Godly woman of faith, showed Joanne the love that she desperately craved. These were foster parents, but were the real parents she had needed. Between these parents and her faith in God, she got through her childhood and the hard times.

Joanne made a lot of mistakes as a young person, especially having children at an early age. As a young adult, she married for the right reasons, wanting to take care of her kids and going to a good church, but she felt like she was playing all the parts in her family. Her husband, she would later find out, was attracted to men and would then leave her and their marriage. Her faith seemed to shatter at this point, and not surprisingly, she wanted to give up altogether. Eventually she stopped going to church, and for years she pursued no real relationships with anyone anymore. She went back to college and worked three jobs at any given time. Her children also seemed hurt, because they could see how angry she was at life. Eventually, she met a new neighbor. Initially, Joanne didn't think too much of it until one day she couldn't find her cell phone. The funny thing was, Joanne thought her neighbor had taken her phone, when it was in her purse the whole time. After that, Joanne and her neighbor started walking together almost every night, and she realized that this person was consistent. Being a kid that has bounced around since childhood, she looked for consistency in people, people who chose to do the right thing in their life and encouraged this behavior in others. It didn't take long for her to wake up. What she realized was that she had chosen the wrong path, yet she desired to be back in church again, doing what God had called her to do for her children and to believe once again in His grace. As you can see, with a discombobulated life and abuse that was not only repetitive but very disturbing, God can pull us through these rough circumstances. Today Joanne is the mother of two and is still involved in her local church, but is willing to let God use her testimony for His glory. For so long she, like many of us, was overcome with shame and guilt, and God says that He has taken all our pain, guilt, and shame away.

Blinded

I endured two eye surgeries after almost losing my eye ... By God's grace, today, I still have my eyesight in my right eye! The funny thing is, when I was a young kid I shot myself in the eye with a pellet gun. To this day, I can remember running into the house and screaming to my mom to help me. She asked what was wrong, and I told her the pellet bounced off something and it came back and went into my eye. Sure enough, she looked at my eye and squeezed the steel pellet out of my eye, where it fell right onto the kitchen floor. Looking back, I should have been wearing my safety glasses, but no, I was too cool for that – not that it would have been 'cool' to have one less eye or be blind for the rest of my life.

In this story – without modern technology and an amazing retinal surgeon – I would not be able to see and would be completely blind in my right eye. One day when I was surfing down at the jetty rocks and after catching a wave, I headed down the line. I did a top turn and then decided to kick out of the wave and tried to catch my board in the air. The wind blew the board back into my face, and the fin went into my eyeball. Talk about trying not to panic when you cannot see out of your eye and your other eye can see blood dripping down. After paddling into shore and asking some friends if I was ok, they all agreed that I should go to the hospital as soon as possible. You know your injury is bad when friends look at you, cringe, and look away. The life guard and the ambulance that showed up all agreed that the severity of the injury needed to be evaluated at the hospital.

Fortunately, one of my friends called my dad, and he immediately came to the beach. He took me to the hospital. I was reminded of the Apostle Paul when he was blinded on the Road to Damascus. That day my eye was blinded by a surfboard on a wave to the inside. However, God would search the inside of my heart. I remember pleading with God for Him to save my eyesight. A serious eye laceration is shocking for a young guy, or anyone for that matter, to go through. When I got to the hospital, the doctor said, "I have good news, and I have bad news. The bad news is you may lose your eye and sight. The good news is we can hopefully save your eye, and you'll be able to see. We are going to have to do emergency surgery first thing in the morning." Coming to grips with the fact that I could lose my eyesight is something that hopefully most will not have to experience. If you have ever been in a situation where you desperately need something, then this story is for you. We all need Jesus. He is the something that everyone needs; He provides salvation. We have good news and bad news in life as well. Ultimately, the good news is that we have Jesus Christ if we have accepted Him into our hearts. The bad news is that we may have hardships to go through. Whenever we go through a hardship of any kind, He is there each step of the way in our life, even to the point of our death.

Not too long ago, I was given the news of a cousin who passed away, and then not much later, another cousin passed away from cancer. A very close member of my family had cancer, one of the people I work with is going through cancer treatment, and another close friend, who is a pastor, was also just diagnosed with bone cancer. After typing all of this you can imagine that we all should be thankful for the life that God has given us all. Life is very fragile, and we are not promised tomorrow. This reminds me that we are to be thankful for each day God gives us to live here on earth. What are you thankful for? Think about how much God loves you even in the times of hurt, desperation, brokenness, and pain. Jesus came to rescue us from all of our pain.

From the depths of despair, O Lord, I call for your help.
Hear my cry, O Lord. Pay attention to my prayer.

Lord, if you kept a record of our sins,
who, O Lord, could ever survive?
But you offer forgiveness, that we might learn to fear you.

I am counting on the Lord; yes, I am counting on him.
I have put my hope in his word. Psalm 130:1-5 (NLT)

CHAPTER THREE

The Boy

Chad remembers as a three-year-old how this little girl across the street would touch him in areas that were not appropriate. He would feel guilty and ashamed, but when he looked around, he did not see the love of his mother. His mother loved him dearly, but she was never around. This boy's father could not understand why she would run away from her family and problems when things would get tough. One in six boys have been molested in their youth. Each year, 16-17% of boys are molested – how sad is this statistic?[2] God, however, can even use such horrific things in a person's past to help them set others free of their mental and physical bondage of sexual sin. Chad's story continues with his personal struggles and with his perceptions of women. Later in life, he would also be abused by a teenage girl that constantly forced him to do illicit acts. You may be thinking to yourself, I must hold onto my shame or guilt, and the truth is: You don't have to! God paid the penalty for the perpetrator's sin and for your guilt. Guilt is a tool of the devil and does not come from our God, who loves us and heals us. Later in life Chad was healed by the grace of God and is now married.

Forgiveness is something that begins by going to God. So

---

[2] Dube, S.R., Anda, R.F., Whitfield, C.L., et al. (2005). Long-term consequences of childhood sexual abuse by gender of victim. American Journal of Preventive Medicine, 28, 430-438.

often people hold onto bitterness, and bitterness is like an acid that eats its own container. When a person harbors bitterness, it continues to destroy them and not the other person. God talks about restoration and healing throughout the Bible and the importance of forgiveness. Part of forgiveness means calling upon God for personal healing. In the Bible there is a word, baptism. In the very beginning of the book of Acts, "[the Apostle] Peter replied, "Each of you must repent of your sins and turn to God and be baptized in the name of Jesus Christ for the forgiveness of your sins." Acts 2:38a (NLT)

When we hold onto unforgiveness, it holds us back from personal healing. The word baptism means cleansing, and it signifies purity from bitterness, hatred, anger, and things that many people struggle with after being a victim of someone else's sin. When we turn to God for forgiveness, it purifies our life. Even the Apostle John told people to repent of their sins and turn to God for forgiveness. God's unfailing love can heal the deepest wounds in one's life.

After Jesus Christ's resurrection, He commanded His disciples to baptize new converts (Matthew 28:19).

> In the Christian faith, baptism is defined as dying and rising with Christ, signifying the death of their old, past life and the beginning of their new life and journey of faith in Jesus.

> What shall we say then? Are we to continue in sin that grace may abound? By no means! How can we who died to sin still live in it? Do you not know that all of us who have been baptized into

Christ Jesus were baptized into his death? We were buried therefore with him by baptism into death, in order that, just as Christ was raised from the dead by the glory of the Father, we too might walk in newness of life. Romans 6:1-4 (ESV)

Having been buried with him in baptism, in which you were also raised with him through faith in the powerful working of God, who raised him from the dead. Colossians 2:12 (ESV)

Baptism also signifies the filling in a person's heart of God's Holy Spirit, a clean conscience before God. Many people see the outward expression of baptism, however, this confirmation process truly is the inside seal of God's spirit. Baptism is often called an outward and physical sign of an inward and spiritual grace. His presence is always guaranteed in your life, if you allow Him. Our prayer, as believers, is the desire to share the truth with others – God awaits faithful people to come be a part of a community of believers that's free from ridicule, condemnation, and judgment of their past. The past is just that, the past. That's why they call today the present; it's a gift. If a person were to drive a car, it would not make much sense to drive looking in their rearview mirrors. Eventually, they would crash. That's why God gives us a windshield of opportunity, to see a small picture of where He is leading us.

Sinking in the Mud

It's easy to know how selfish a person is when you're on the receiving end of someone being selfish. It started off when my mom took my friend, Kevin, and I over toward the back of the adjacent neighborhood to do some shopping. Kevin and I, a couple of ten-year old's, thought it would be best to throw some rocks out into the swamp mud. You know that type of mud, when it's a very low tide, it's just like quicksand. Kevin thought it would be a great idea to see how deep the mud really was. Before I knew it, he was waist deep in the mud, and he started to panic. He started screaming for me to come out there and help him. Meanwhile, I thought to myself, "I'm not the smallest kid around, and if I go help rescue him we'll both sink to our death." Like any smart kid would do, I thought to myself, "What would I do?" I yelled at Kevin to stay calm, and then I went to find some rope I could throw to him. Meanwhile, he thought he could just swim out of the mud. Looking back at it now, I just laugh about how muddy Kevin got, but it was no laughing matter at the time. I never did find any rope, and it ended up taking me a little time to get enough rocks in the bottom of the mud for him to grip onto, and he slowly crawled into shore. He was covered in mud and there was no way my mom wanted to take him home in our truck, but like any awesome mom would do, she took us two muddy kids home anyway.

God always seems to throw us a rope and get us out of our troubles. Sometimes God pulls us instantly out of our mess, but sometimes His timing is different than ours. Sometimes it is a slow, forward progress that seems to stretch us a lot or seems overwhelming, but by taking us out of our comfort zone and through these troubling times, He develops our faith and character. This ultimately draws us closer to Him.

When the Rope Swing Breaks

Sometimes God allows you to fall so that you learn. Have you ever heard a parent say the following statements "Be careful," "Please listen to me," or "I am not sure that's a good idea?" These comments are a fact of life. As most young kids do, I had a fascination with swinging in the air – it's a sense of exhilaration, excitement, freedom, and falling. Like I said, I was always the kid on the block that everyone used as the test pilot or guinea pig. I didn't mind being that person, because I've always been a risk taker. There are educated risks, and on one memorable day, I would have much rather passed up the opportunity of falling.

Over near the interstate, there was a place with about a five to ten-foot hill. For some reason, a tree was growing on top of this hill area. The great thing was, they started to remove the dirt from the edge, and you could rope swing off the edge of the dirt over the cliff. Ten feet doesn't seem very far, but when you're swinging at a high rate of speed, while you're coming to the edge, and you fall because the swing breaks, it doesn't feel very good when you flop on the ground. These are the kind of impacts that knock the wind out of you. The fall was so hard I made a wincing kind of noise. All my so-called friends' reactions were the following, "Aww, Troy fell so hard!", or "Man I bet that hurt." I just thought to myself, "I have to get up, and I can't say it hurt at all." All I knew was it hurt but not as bad as the hard fall of my ego from the embarrassment. Have you ever just really wanted to cry after getting hurt but were too concerned about what others would think about you?

There were many times that I had fallen as a kid, but I

remember the time when I fell in the backyard from a rope swing I had built out of my dog's wire leash. Due to my body growth, I exceeded the weight limits of this leash. Therefore, in mid-swing, it sent me into the top of our sharp metal fence. I thank God for that fence. When that swing broke that fence was what broke my fall. Meanwhile, my jean pants leg got caught on the fence, and I was hanging upside down from the fence. I couldn't get myself down and was yelling to my friend, "Help! Get me down!" At that moment, it appeared that I would come crashing to the ground, but much like a person's faith in God, it's when you really believe you're going to fall that God makes Himself available to you, even in the most uncomfortable situations. He gives you the hope to get back up when you feel like crying or quitting. He gives you the strength when you feel broken. He gives you a fence to catch you when you fall.

Don't Play with Fire

Before we start this story, I would like to share with you about clothing. Just the other day, I was in the local jail sharing a story with prisoners of when you wear the clothes of pride, bitterness, shame, and guilt. These are the type of clothes that make it very heavy for a person to move around. One time, I was speaking at Radford University, telling students the importance of breaking addictive behavior. The Bible says we are God's children. As a child of God, we would never want to suffocate our lives with the guilt and shame of our past. God's Word clearly says He makes all things new. We can let go and give our shame and guilt to God. If a person had a young child, no one in their right mind would continue to pile clothes on that young child, because eventually the child would suffocate. This is why God removes the guilt, shame, pride, and bitterness giving us the opportunity to live life to the fullest so we do not suffocate under the heavy clothing of guilt and shame that some of us still try to wear or put on.

> A thief comes to steal, kill, and destroy. But I came
> so that my sheep will have life and so that they will
> have everything they need. John 10:10 (GWT)

As God puts people into your life, think if they are people that are tearing you down or building you up. Jesus came to give us life! The enemy comes to steal it away.

As a young boy, I loved learning about fishing, hunting, and fire. One day, down near Shore Drive, I was with another young friend of mine, who had a fascination with fire. We went into the local convenience store, and he picked up a few matches despite my hesitation. Then we headed back to where my mom's friend lived, because everyone was hanging out. My friend then showed me this awesome trick called match flicking. It's when you take your index finger and the match head, and you flick it off the match book and it turns into a flaming projectile. Wow! This is awesome if you are under 10 by the way. No harm is done if the match lands in the dirt or in the water, but on this day, the match would land in someone's yard that had lots of pine straw right near their deck. I didn't think much about it until about an hour later when several fire trucks came down the road, and there was a knock at the front door, and then the doorbell rang. The fire department asked if they had seen a little red-headed boy, and my mother responded, "My son has red hair." She described me, and the fire chief said, "He fits our description." I remember coming down the stairs and talking to the local fire chief who explained that someone had seen two young boys walking through the neighbor's yard before seeing the fire which had burnt up part of the neighbor's deck attached to their home. The only words I could say were, "I didn't do it, but I know who might have." Instead of being a tattle-tale, I ended up getting in trouble for the whole thing. Looking back at it, I'm glad I had to go to the fire prevention class. It taught me a lot about fire, but more importantly, the dangers that it poses.

With that said, now I would like to share with you what the Bible says. It talks about how sin ultimately separates us from God. When a person continues to choose things that do not honor God, it leads them away from Him and down the wrong path. Sin is like fire, and it will burn you if you mess around with it. Sin is like a fire that no one puts out. Once it is out of control it is usually too late, and whatever is on fire burns down. This is much like the enemy in our life. He wants to see you burned down, burnt out, and ruined. Ultimately, I learned that having better friends who cared about being together and having fellowship is the best way to keep you from a life of sin and making bad decisions. This is called accountability. For a long time, I heard a lot of "Christianeze," or what some would call church language, that only people in the church could understand. Later, I would find out that accountability is for encouraging people in their "walks" (better known as relationships) with Christ. Accountability is having a support group or someone to be transparent with and hold you responsible for your choices – both of which are essential to a person's faith.

CHAPTER FOUR

Why Suicide?

The stories of a new friend and of a dear friend who is gone.

Post-its—just leave one behind

Day of Post-its: A while back there was a movement going around where people were giving away Christian Post-it notes and quotes to open conversations. I eventually ran into a person who read one that was in the bathroom at a local restaurant that gave him hope. "Man, this post-it that I read inside the restroom was just what I needed. I felt completely hopeless today, and after reading this post-it, it was as if God left it right there to minister to me."

Here are a few Post-Its I stumbled across, and these Post-Its have encouraged me, and they made me laugh!

- PIBCAC – sometimes we can all be this. The acronym stands for Problem Is Between Chair and Computer
- What do you call a deer with no eyes? I have no eye-deer (idea) either.
- If you worry, why pray? And if you pray, why worry?

Not sure which Post-It this guy stumbled across! But any of these could correlate to our lives, because sometimes we can be the problem, other times we have no idea where God is leading us next, and why worry? God has everything in His hands. He holds the future.

This last Post-It is one that can be a reminder for us all.

- The Word of God will keep you from sin! Or sin will keep you from the Word of God!

Let's be honest – we all read a post-it note when we see one. Give this a try – it can't really hurt anything, and it may just save a life or a soul. Maybe your post-it finds a person on the brink of suicide or maybe it finds a person on the verge of adultery – either way, God can use your post-it to save that person. Maybe the person just needs inspiration, or maybe they just need to hear a kind word – let that be God's Holy Word.

Suicide

The story of a man who tried to commit suicide on three separate occasions: first, he put a gun to his head and pulled the trigger, but the primer had a dent on it, and the gun failed to fire. Next, he was driving over 100 miles an hour and tried to drive off a bridge, but his car hit the guardrail instead, keeping him from going off the bridge. When the police arrived, he lied to them about his intentions and said he dozed off. Finally, the police came to his house, and they found a noose around his neck - his neighbor had called the police. When they arrived, they asked, "You seem like a really nice guy, why do you want to give up on life?" He responded, "I've always struggled with depression, and I just want to give up and quit. I don't have anyone." Needless to say, the police saved him from his intentions, and today this person is doing well because he found the Lord.

Anyone can die at any moment. What are we doing this moment that will give God glory and help others in need? This is a great question that people often ask themselves. One afternoon I got a call from a friend, letting me know that a piece of glass fell off a platform in a local hardware store and cut through his arm. He is well today, but at the time, the doctors thought he would possibly lose his arm or die.

Another man I knew told me the story of when he fell from scaffolding thirteen stories high, landing with both arms out in front of him. He crushed more bones than the orthopedic surgeon had ever seen. With God's help, they put his arms back together, and he is expected to have almost a full recovery. Wow! Think of all the things we see and hear each day. Hopefully you see God's hand at work in the lives of those who are survivors.

Someone asked me what would those survivors do on the tv shows if they found a bag full of money in the amount of a million dollars or more? When a person is on an island in the middle of nowhere a bag full of money really does not mean anything. Some dear friends of mine have more financial provision than most people will ever see in their lifetime, yet they all say the same thing, "Having a lot does not make you any different than anyone else." True, except that they have more to be responsible for managing. The Bible talks about being a good steward of what we have been given. But someone who does not know, and then does something wrong, will be punished only lightly. "When someone has been given much, much will be required in return;

and when someone has been entrusted with much, even more will be required." Luke 12:48 (NLT)

Think about people who you see just frivolously waste money or any type of resources. It is a lack of responsibility. We are called to practice good stewardship and use wisdom as we make decisions and choices, especially when our decisions make a direct impact on other people's lives. Think of those who use drugs. You see the drugs ruin their lives. Knowing that when we have a desire to give charity to this individual, we know deep down that it may enable them to continue in the lifestyle that they are choosing. Therefore, pray about how God would want you to help this individual before you give them anything.

It seems like people today, including pastors and those in the church, can struggle with depression. When we do not have fellowship, it can lead to people taking things into their own hands. One year, while I was serving as an academic advisor at a major university, there was a student who came into my office. He shared with me a recent break-up with his girlfriend, and how empty and lost he felt. Little did I know, this would turn into an opportunity to share the hope that only God can give when you lose a person in your life that you deeply care for. On this day, my office received a phone call from his parents about their concern for their son. This is where I had to make tough decisions to commit or pull away from the situation.

Later that week, I was asked to visit this young man in the hospital. He had attempted suicide and wound up in the hospital. I prayed about the issue, left work, and went to visit him with a gallon of ice cream and a box of cookies. Yes, this seemed odd, but God doesn't ask you to do something only when it is convenient for you. God shows up when we surrender to Him and allow Him to lead us. While at the hospital, he and I shared a lot of things about life and how selfish taking your own life is. A person can never see the impact on those left behind when he or she takes their own life. In this particular instance, I shared with him the most important aspect of life –my faith in Christ, and I asked him if he had faith as well. He said he was finally ready to surrender his life to Christ.

After a few years had passed, I learned that he went back to his country where he is now faithfully serving the Lord. I was wondering how this all came to fruition, so he shared the story when his family invited me to visit them in Costa Rica, blessing me by allowing me to stay at their home on the beach. They could see a joy in my life that was unexplainable. He asked, "How can you be so sure God leads you?" I said, "This is faith. Believing in something you don't see, but knowing He is there." During this journey, we don't always know what is next.

Oftentimes, we have a mindset of 'seeing is believing.' Having something tangible gives us peace, but God consistently calls us as believers to trust and believe. In our Christian walk, sometimes believing is seeing – seeing God at work in our lives and knowing that it is not mere coincidence.

What a blessing it is to know where some of us are now, because someone shared their faith in Christ with us. Sometimes people think the worst of things, but we are called to focus on the good and celebrate life. Hopefully, we celebrate the good things in life and do not dwell on the bad circumstances or past mistakes. Love hopes and thinks the best of others. Jesus told people things they did not want to hear all throughout scripture, but He still loved them. John 8:32b (ESV) says, "The Truth will set you free." We can be trapped by our own false motives, false perceptions, and unrealistic beliefs.

I may never fully understand this next story. The night I received a call on a mission trip to Costa Rica was the same night I learned my friend Jack had passed away. Whether intentional or unintentional, I know that he is in a better place with the Lord. Now some would say that if you take your life, how would you go to heaven? The better question is, if God has saved a person, does He still give us the most dangerous gift that mankind has ever received: free will? We have the choice to choose life and in some cases to choose death.

No one, hopefully, would ever wish death upon a person, and when death is self-inflicted there are many questions that cannot be answered on this side of Heaven. You might ask yourself, at this point, why anyone would share this. By sharing this with you, hopefully this can provide you some insight on a person's life that changed mine. When we lose someone, our life changes. Life here on earth is constantly changing. The only constant is God and His love for us. Jack's love for God and for others was unbelievable. He would always ask me to question what I believed. He even reminded me to be careful of pride, not that I understood this fact at the time. One afternoon I finally asked him what he meant by that, and he said spiritual pride.

I never understood that concept as a young Christian, early in my faith. Now I completely understand that God has no place for pride. He wants us to walk in humility. People who walk in humility possess an exceptional quality and characteristic of God and His nature. Even when writing my dissertation at Virginia

Tech, I was reminded, humility comes before honor. That is what Proverbs 18:12 describes. Humility, some would define as letting others speak for you. If your actions are humble and righteous, then those around you will speak for your worth. One of my fondest moments of my friendship with Jack was when Jack listened to me for hours while I shared about my personal relationship with God and my struggles with doubt at times. He taught me about Jewish culture and faith.

> Haughtiness goes before destruction; humility
> precedes honor. Proverbs 18:12 (ESV)

At first, I wasn't sure specifically what I liked about Jack, but I could see that he was gracious and compassionate. He would challenge me to possess the quality of being humble and love others no matter what they had gone through in their past. Now that I look back, I realize that this is, in fact, an area where many of us can struggle. We are continually wanting to receive the honor, the glory, and the praise, when God deserves all these things and more. He has given us life. Our joy as Christians can be found in surrendering our lives to Him to serve others for His glory, not for ours. This was the life Jack lived. He loved to serve us Jewish delicacies and a few sodas every now and then. Did I mention that he loved video games? But better yet, he loved Virginia Tech football, and he loved his church family where he treasured the fellowship of Christian believers.

> What good fellowship we once enjoyed as we walked
> together to the house of God. Psalm 55:14 (NLT)

It seems like God has brought me on many trips throughout my life, some trips I have taken alone. In others, it seemed, God allowed someone to join me along the journey, and in some cases, the adventures. The real journey in life is one of faith. One day, I bought a ticket to visit the big island of Hawaii. I was living on another island, which most people have heard of, called Oahu. Living life to the fullest at this point in my life, as many surfers would say, it was truly the endless summer – perfect weather and I loved the island culture. Most of the locals realized that I had adopted what they called the true aloha spirit, and that is sharing true Aloha. "Aloha is Love" and this can only come from God "Akua." I learned this while surfing on the south shore at Kaiser bowls.

I really enjoyed surfing around the island, but I had come to the realization that God put me on this island for a far greater purpose: to pray for people, help people in need, and serve the local community in any way that I could during my time spent there. On my flight to the Big Island, Hawaii, I remember running into this military guy that we'll call Jay. I landed at the airport, not expecting to just walk out onto the runway with an open-air setting. I then went to the local rental car place where I had reservations, and I looked over at this military guy who was staring at me. I introduced myself, said I was here for a quick vacation, and asked him why he was here and where he was heading. He had a sort of blank stare on his face. He said he really wasn't sure, and that all he had was a backpack.

Normally, I don't ask people if they need a ride, but seeing as how the rental car company had some pretty steep prices on the rest of their cars, I offered Jay a ride. I didn't want him Jay walking (pun intended). But to my surprise, he gladly accepted my offer, so he could get to where he was heading. I wasn't sure whether he thought I was a little out there, but then I started to think to myself, maybe he's a little out there that he would accept the offer. About an hour and a half into our drive around the island, I couldn't help but notice over every high bridge we went over he asked, "How far do you think it is down?" I told him I wasn't sure, but it looks like a long way and asked why he asked. His response was always, "Just wondering."

I finally got around to asking him, "Why are you here?" He was kind of vague, said he'd always been interested in seeing volcanoes. I said, "Great. Let's drive to where the active volcano is." He said sure. Once we visited the volcano, I asked him where to go next. He admitted to me he didn't have reservations anywhere. I did and started to wonder who takes a one-way ticket to an Island in the South Pacific? Oh, that's right, that is how I ended up here myself. At the time, I was working for the Aston Waikiki beach hotel back on Oahu, and they had set me up with a nice place on the Big Island. I told him I was sure there was plenty of room where I was staying. I asked, "Do you want to see if there are rooms available? If not, I have an extra bedroom you can stay in."

At this point, I was hungry, so we went back to Kona Kailua to eat. Afterwards, I continued to get to know Jay, and I realized that something just didn't seem right. I didn't want to be too intrusive, so I used some discernment. Waiting for God's perfect timing is always the best. We went back to the place I had booked, and he fell asleep fast in the guest room. Jay had a few drinks, and after our trip around the island, he was tired and out quick. Meanwhile, I prayed and wrote in my journal.

The next morning, I woke up about 4:30. I couldn't help but notice Jay's backpack, which was unzipped, was almost empty, but it had a pen, some paper, and a bottle of alcohol. Strange that there were no clothes or anything. I thought, "Why would you take a trip with a lot of alcohol, a pen and a paper?" When he got up later that morning he said, "What are your plans for today?" I told him I was going to continue to travel around the island and visit some of the local churches. He then told me he needed to use the computer and told me he had changed his mind about some things.

After a deep conversation and me sharing my testimony of how God had changed my life, he said I reminded him of his parents. I drove him back to the airport, and while I parked, he shared something with me, that really impacted me. He said, "I came to the island with a one-way ticket." It didn't really dawn on me until he said, "Maybe God put you here for me." I didn't really think much of it until he started walking away and at that point I remembered him asking about the height of every bridge. Maybe God has a trip planned for you to share God's love, grace, and compassion to a person whose mind may have been set on ending their life. Either way prayerfully Jay is doing well.

Since we believe human testimony, surely,
we can believe the greater testimony
that comes from God. And God has testified
about his Son. 1 John 5:9 (NLT)

Traveling with Tom

You never know when you're going to get a random call from a close friend saying, "Hey, I really just want to end my life."

Some people struggle with depression their whole lives. I never knew what that looked like until I dealt with it through one of my close friends. He said he needed prayer, and I remember saying, "Well, I'm right here." If someone needs prayer, just be bold enough to pray for them right at that moment. You may not know the right words, but God can use you. "[God's] Word will not return void." Isaiah 55:11 (KJV) Anytime you use Scripture to talk to someone, it will have some result for good. It may not be immediately apparent, but it is at least planting that seed in another person's life. Your silence out of fear often times could be a missed opportunity. As a person steps out in faith and trusts, God gives them the words to speak. Romans 12:6, "If you preach, just preach God's Message, nothing else; if you help, just help, don't take over" (the Message).

Tom and I were on the road, heading across the country. I wasn't quite sure where we were even heading, but I knew for some reason that this was where I was supposed to be, helping someone in need. Tom needed me for emotional support and, in this case, spiritual. Our lives are constantly in flux. Many people's lives take a change for the worse, and this is when people really need you. There are many circumstances that factor into the way God uses a person. While typing this chapter, I received a phone call from a dear friend in California. He reminded me that we are all called to share the Gospel. The Bible talks about the Kingdom of God, it expresses Christ in us and through us, showing people about Him. We are often asked the question, "What can I do?"

The real answer is putting our faith in God and trusting His Holy Spirit to lead us in doing His work. This ties into the story of Tom. The Lord had me on this trip to share with Tom the importance of being a father and not to give up on life. So often we want to just quit on our journey of faith. I'm reminded of the Apostle Paul who went through persecution, beatings, trials, and tribulation, while trusting God. Sometimes we need a person to look us straight in the eye and say, "Get your head together." The only person that can get your head together is God. Maybe it would have been better if I told him to give his head to God. He is the only One Who can give us peace in our hearts and minds. God's Word says, "Do not be conformed to this world, but be transformed by the renewal of your mind, that by testing you may discern what is the will of God, what is good and acceptable and perfect" Romans 12:2 (ESV). Christ is the One who renews our minds and puts our heads back together. Someone once stated something like this, "God gives you two hands. One to receive God's blessings, and the other to give His blessings to others." Sometimes our blessing is just giving ourselves to the Lord and allowing Him the opportunity to use us for His glory.

Hopefully this gives those questioning a reason why God keeps them alive; it's because God has a purpose and plan for your life. When we trust God, He can use us in any situation.

Set free from acid – the story of Jimmy

You never know when you're going to get a phone call from a mother in a crisis over her son. I received such a call one strange night. I was asked to go to someone's house at the north end of the beach to visit this young man. I was told to just go to the door and knock. Being as bold as God has made me, I figured why not? So, I did, not expecting what I was about to see. I found a young man who seemed to be somewhat intoxicated. He told me to enter and then asked if he could share a story with me. I said sure.

Two hours later, I was still listening to him. To make a long story short: He asked me whether I had ever done acid. I told him no. He told me his story of doing too much acid one evening. He said he remembered falling asleep, and when he woke up, he remembered his feet dangling over the edge of the bed. He said the strange part about it was when he looked over the edge of his bed, all he saw was complete darkness. He wanted to know whether Satan was real. He explained that there were pink neon pentagrams lit up, and he remembers a voice saying, "Isn't this what you wanted? A life of bliss, drugs, and doing whatever you want?" He said he wasn't sure where he stood "with the whole God thing." But this night he said he could really use some prayer. I asked him why he was telling me this story, and he said he knew Satan was real and that Satan wants to destroy him and everyone else. I said yes this is true. The enemy's job is to steal, kill, and destroy. And the darkness that he was describing is like eternal separation from God. God's Word clearly says that He separates the light from the darkness. I told him about my life before I had given my life to Jesus. I asked myself, "Why am I even here? Is this helping in any way?" Then I asked Jimmy, "Are you going to stay here tonight?"

He replied, "I'm going to take a bike trip and just keep going south to Florida." I followed up with, "Well, where are you going to go?" He said, "I don't know. I'm just going to keep pedaling south, and when I get to the end of the state I will find a boat to hop on and ask if I can ride along." When a person is lost, they don't know where they are going or what they are doing. There's no plan. God's Word says for those who are saved, He has a plan for us. When I asked Jimmy to pray with me, he gladly accepted. I remember my last words before I left his house that night, and the last time I would ever see this young man, "God, rescue him from himself and the bad decisions he continues to make." He prayed with me, and before I left he said "Troy, thanks for coming by. Thanks for just taking the time to spend with someone you didn't know and share about God's love for me. For that I'm very thankful." I left and prayed that the Lord would find him along his journey.

The Story of Rick

Well, I would love to have his perspective of this story. Maybe one day this book will be in his hands, and he will be able to share with me. He was such a blessing to me. One afternoon driving down a road called Shore Drive I noticed a young man walking along with a pretty large size backpack, like the ones the military issues. Needless to say, I felt as though it was put on my heart to pull over and ask him where he was headed. He looked at me and he said, "Why do you ask?" I said, because in either direction it's a long hike. His response was, I'm heading to the resort area, do you know where that is? I said, "Yeah, it's about another three miles down the road. If you want a ride, I'll give you one." He said sure. I was thinking to myself, "I wonder who this guy is." He just started to open up and talk to me along the road. He said he was in the military, and he didn't really go into detail about his job, but I was glad that he was a soldier who serves our country. At the time, I was thankful he didn't have a gun in his bag to hold me up. It's funny how we think of these things, and some of these reservations are what keep us from sharing our stories or picking up random people on the side of the road, and sometimes for good reason this day and age. Sometimes we are trapped by the fear of the unknown. However, in some circumstances if you are ok with helping a person and you are not alone or a man that knows Jesus or is not concerned about any bad outcomes, then go for it! Ladies please do not pick up random guys off the road!

Once we got to the resort area, he had asked me to join him for some food. All I remember is exchanging numbers with him and calling him three years later. During that phone call we started talking about our lives, and then he explained to me that he started working down in Florida helping out with a Christian organization. He said something about, "Do you remember that prayer that you prayed for me?" I honestly can't remember the prayer, but I know it was probably something like, "God bless this man in his journey of faith, and may your hand be upon him in this season of life and open up opportunity for him to share the Gospel." There have been a lot of stories like this that I don't necessarily remember all the intricate details of, but God knows every aspect of our lives: our waking up, our going to sleep, our falls, and when He picks us back up. Even when I look at our daughter, Gracelynn, she reminds me that it is one small, simple step of faith, and at times we get tripped up by the obstacles in life, called toys, or even our own feet.

So often we can be held back and become captives of fear. I was just reading in a book that addressed what really matters. I believe what matters today more than ever is reaching people who are skeptical or hurt. Those people that society would consider broken people. When a person is a Christian we help serve the communities around us by reaching out to people and sharing the truth of God's love with them. There's an old saying that people don't care how much you have to say until they know how much you care. One way that we can show the truth is to model Jesus. This is exemplified through compassion, mercy, and giving people the hope of Christ. Someone once stated that I was a very pragmatic individual who is defined by my creative thinking and passion for the community. He said through preaching and teaching and writing God will shine through me.

For a long time, I really struggled with accepting what some would say the call on my life was. Many people can struggle with having a clear vision, idea, or picture of what they would like to be involved in for the Glory of God. One way in which we can understand or recognize our talent is by communicating with those who we love. As a person shares their heart, God guides our footsteps as well. Our vision has to first start by being focused on Christ before moving on to the next step. The Gospel in Matthew 9:35 seems to be saying if you are sharing the Gospel, share hope and serve people. "Jesus went through all the towns and villages, teaching in their synagogues, proclaiming the good news of the kingdom and healing every disease and sickness." Matthew 9:35 (NIV). When people see acts of His amazing love, it connects communities and people to a God of amazing grace!

Dead to Sin, Alive in Christ

On the way to Charlotte, North Carolina to visit a friend I remember sensing that I should call this man, Mitch, who I met in the airport a while back. After picking up the phone and dialing

I remembered thinking it was strange. "What am I going to say? Will he remember me?" Sure enough, he did pick up, and gave me his address and told me to please stop by. Wow, to my surprise he thought maybe one day he might hear from me. Once I pulled up in the driveway he came out to meet me, and then invited me into his home. He was the type of guy that is straight and to the point. He asked where I was heading, and I told him Florida. He then asked why. "To visit my Grandparents and a friend." He then jumped over to the next topic which was if I was saved. "What does that really mean," I asked him. He said, "Have you given your life to Jesus?" "Yes," I responded, "but I have not been living my life like I have given my life to Him." He asked, "How so?" "I have not been being honest with this friend of mine that I know lies to me." He then said, "What are you going to do?" I said, "I am going to confront that person and make amends and forgive them."

Mitch was such a bold person. He was very outspoken about his faith and trust in God. I asked how was he so certain. He said, "Look at my life now." He was saved at an outreach event twenty years ago. He stated he needed a change from the life he was living. He was drinking heavily, running after all the ladies, and being dishonest. I asked Mitch, "How did you know you were lost?" He said, "That is a great question." He asked me if I had ever read Romans chapter 6, and I said, "Not lately if at all." He said, "If we say we are Christians then we are dead to sin and alive to Christ." Then he asked me to read 1 Corinthians 6:9-20 out of a Bible he had in his home.

Or do you not know that the
unrighteous will not inherit
the kingdom of God? Do not be deceived:
neither the sexually immoral,
nor idolaters, nor adulterers,
nor men who practice homosexuality,
nor thieves, nor the greedy,
nor drunkards, nor revilers,
nor swindlers will inherit the kingdom of God.
And such were some of you.
But you were washed, you were sanctified,
you were justified in the name of the Lord Jesus
Christ and by the Spirit of our God.

"All things are lawful for me,"
but not all things are helpful.
"All things are lawful for me,"
but I will not be dominated by anything.
"Food is meant for the stomach
and the stomach for food"—
and God will destroy both one
and the other. The body is not meant for
sexual immorality, but for the Lord,
and the Lord for the body.
And God raised the Lord and
will also raise us up by his power.
Do you not know that your bodies
are members of Christ? Shall I then take
the members of Christ and make them

members of a prostitute? Never!
Or do you not know that he
who is joined to a prostitute
becomes one body with her?
For, as it is written,
"The two will become one flesh."
But he who is joined to the Lord
becomes one spirit with him.
Flee from sexual immorality.
Every other sin a person commits is outside the body,
but the sexually immoral person
sins against his own body. Or do you not know
that your body is a temple of the Holy Spirit within you,
whom you have from God?
You are not your own, for you were bought with a price.
So glorify God in your body.
1 Corinthians 6:9-20 (ESV)

After reading this I knew I needed to make some major changes in my life. Just knowing that Mitch cared enough to share his testimony and life with me gave me a whole new perspective for the Bible and God's Word. When we are seeking God, He will direct our path and sometimes even lead us off the interstate to visit a friend.

Thin Ice

Growing up in our neighborhood, I came to the realization that I do not float. I was your typical young kid during the winter with all my friends – hoping for snow. I was the kid that was the risk taker, or at least the one in this story. I walked out on the ice of the very same canal that I could not jump over on my bike. Back then it seemed like winters were under 30 degrees. It made you wonder how people could live in this weather; you had to put on a heavy winter coat just to stay warm.

On a side note, it is interesting that people who live up North say, "Wow, it gets so hot down South," and the people down South say, "Wow, it gets so cold up North." Where I grew up, we had occasional snow, and sometimes ice would form over the lakes and canals if it was cold enough for an extended period. The ice would form, and you could even walk on the ice when the winter was cold enough. On this day I decided to test the ice for all my friends. I remember them saying, "Troy will do it." Well, I sure did. I walked out about 10-feet from the shore, and I remember hearing it start to crack. In the next breath, I broke through the ice with a splash.

I remember the other kids all running away, some of them were laughing, and the others didn't know what to do until I yelled out for help. Two of my friends got together to reach out for me over the edge of the ice, hand-in-hand. It was a miracle I did not end up going into shock or drowning that day. I survived another near-death experience, and yes, around water again. Looking back, it seems very odd that I still enjoy being a waterman as much as I do today, despite all the near-death experiences that have taken place in the water throughout my life.

God says in His word, "Perfect love cast out all fear." 1 John 4:18 (ESV). Jesus can help you through any fears. He constantly reminds me that His disciples need not be afraid. It's important to use the common sense that God has given us though. As you can see, God has His hand on our lives from the moment we are conceived. God also gives us a brain to use when testing the integrity of ice or being around water. There is a saying on the beach signs in Hawaii that simply states "When in doubt, don't go out." In other words, do not test the Lord.

The Ducks

One afternoon I gave a skateboard to a kid, and all I could remember were the ducks walking across the street. It was a mama duck and her ducklings followed her in a line. I wasn't sure of the significance at the time, but after giving the skateboard away, I knew that I had given away much more than a skateboard. This young boy's story is like many of the people that I have had the opportunity to share God's grace from inside of the jail within the prison ministry. This young kid told me that his dad got into some trouble and that he could not see him. I asked why, and he told me his dad was in prison. He said he was spending a lot of time with his mom and that this upcoming Christmas he would not be able to have the skateboard he wanted. I told him God provides for our desires and needs in mysterious ways. I got up and ran into the house to grab this skateboard, writing on it, "Your gift from Jesus." I gave him a small book called U-Turn that included the gospel of John. On the bottom of the skateboard I let him know that the best gift we can ever receive is Jesus. I asked him if he knew about Jesus. He said no, but that he would like to learn. I remember praying with this kid, and I told him that "If you confess with your mouth that Jesus is Lord and believe in your heart that God raised him from the dead, you will be saved." Romans 10:9 (ESV). He gave me a high five and said thanks. He appreciated the skateboard and asked, "Who do I tell my mom the skateboard is from?"

I replied, "Tell her to read the bottom of the skateboard. It was a gift from Jesus." He laughed and said, "Good, because then my mom will know I didn't steal it."

You might wonder why I started this story with a momma duck leading her chicks across the street. Each of us, as parents, have the responsibility to lead our children and raise them up in the Lord. This is our first ministry: taking care of our homes by loving our wives first then our children. Men today hopefully will commit to leading and loving their family. We have seen the beginning effects of a Godless society all around us. Hopefully, if you are a parent reading this book, you'll make this commitment to the Lord to pray and read God's Word together as a family. It will make a difference! So, what did it mean to see those ducks following their mother across the road? It's like us following God through the paths of life, and how there can be obstacles at every corner. God will see you through the dangers and the busy streets of life. He gives us directions. It is up to us to decide if we are willing to trust and follow him.

CHAPTER FIVE

The Ten Trials of Troy, One-Four

Brokenness, Humility, and Patience

The gun

The day started like any other. I went to school as usual, but after school I was confronted by the barrel of a .38 revolver on my chest. I'll never forget the words this person told me, "I can kill you right now." Like a smart-alec, I spread my arms and said, "Sure, go ahead. Shoot me." Certainly not what you would tell someone at a moment like this, but at that point in my life, living didn't seem that important. Sometimes, when people are hurting or have some physical or mental anguish, they do not care if they die. That was me at that moment. I'll never forget the feeling of knowing that, "At this moment, if this person pulls the trigger, I'll be dead." The next thing I remember, I reached out and grabbed the gun away from this individual.

Once the gun was in my hand, it was apparent to me by the weight of it that this was a real gun. I was perplexed at the fact that someone had pulled a real gun on me and threatened to kill me. Next, I pointed it at the ground, and everyone backed away from me. Just to make sure it was a real gun, I pulled the trigger, and sure enough, it went off. Thank God, I pointed it at the ground. The people in the neighborhood ran frantically away from the scene. I also recall thinking, "Wow, I have never seen people run this fast in my life."

This was when my own Dad came to the scene. He could not believe just how close his son came to death. My dad was upset I put myself in this situation. I pleaded with him, trying to explain that it was not my fault and let him know that another individual was the one who pulled the gun on me. The thing that surprised me most was that my dad was upset with me and the situation. I thought he would just be thankful that the person didn't kill me. I guess sometimes parents don't know how to react; therefore, it is important for us all to show grace to our parents when they make mistakes. Remember when we do things wrong they forgive us, just like our Heavenly Father forgives us when we make mistakes.

The run

Running away from God, family, and education.

If you have ever visited Virginia Tech, the Jefferson National Forest is very short drive from the campus. You do not want to get lost in this area. On this day, however, after dealing with the loss of my football career at VT, I drove up to the National Forest. As I walked, I carried a rock in my hand – about 4 pounds – not sure what I was going to do with this rock, but when you're upset and frustrated sometimes you just want to throw something. Instead of wasting or throwing my life away, this is where God would show up – a place in the forest where I was completely lost.

God made it clear to me that He is the rock in my life. So here I was, feeling as if life had been taken away, but God was saying, "I gave you your life, and your life is now in me." Your identity cannot be in a sport, a career, another person, or anything other than God. When our identity is in Christ we have hope – otherwise we are hopeless. It's funny how being lost in the woods can sometimes lead you to the place where God finds you. When we are still before God, it allows all the distractions of this world to fade away.

Maybe you're asking yourself at this moment, "What matters in my life?" Hopefully, the following come to mind: 1. Your walk with God, 2. Your family, and 3. Your friends. But when you're at the end of your rope, the only person who is really there is God. When you are in complete isolation, ask yourself what really matters in life. Just ask a person who is incarcerated in the solitary confinement area of the prison and they will tell you about a dark place. Even there, God's love gives a person the peace that he or she needs.

When we come to this realization, it gives hope, and hope does not disappoint. I remember thinking to myself, "How ironic that when you try to run away from God, He meets you right in the very place you would least expect." Now, might I add, I was completely lost in this national forest at this point, and God's Word says very clearly, "I have come to save that which was lost." So here I was, standing in the forest, just me and the Lord. How ironic. It was like God was speaking to my heart and asked, "Troy, are you willing to surrender?" I was not quite sure what was happening at that moment.

Many of us aren't sure what we have to surrender, and God's Word says to surrender our hearts to Him, not just our material possessions. He wants all of you and all you have. This means your life! It is about God's perfect timing and grace. It is about surrendering one's life so that God can use you for His glory. The

Lord led me out of the woods that day, to the dirt road where my truck was parked. As I got back in the truck that afternoon, I knew that I was living for much more than a football career or a college degree.

Meeting God while drowning in Hawaii – as discussed in a previous chapter

I was surfing big waves on the North Shore of Oahu – a very dangerous sport for even the most experienced surfer. After paddling out and getting into position, I took off on a wave, air dropped, dug the rail, and wiped out really bad. After getting pushed under I knew I was in a bad spot. My ears started hurting due to being so deep under the water. Right after climbing my leash back to the surface to catch my breath, a second wave slammed me back down just as deep again– At this point I knew I was close to drowning in the water and realized the similarity to my life. I was drowning in sin as well. God met me, under the water, on the verge of drowning and saved my life in two ways. He got me back to the beach, and He saved me from my sin.

Mom

There are times in a person's life that they may not ever forget. My dad picked up the phone, and I knew something was horribly wrong. He told me, "Your mother has passed away." I remember the emotional pain, yet also the peace of knowing my mom was now free from the earthly body she was constrained in. You see, my mother had a disease called ALS, most people know this as Lou Gehrig's disease. Basically, this disease continues to shut your body down until you succumb. It slowly takes away one's ability to move. Towards the end, it even takes away the ability to breathe on your own.

A friend of mine encouraged me to go see my mother before she passed away. I knew deep down this was the right thing to do, but I was still somewhat apprehensive about seeing my mother in this condition. It would be one of the best memories I would ever have of my mom. When I did see her, I asked my mom if she knew Jesus. She looked at me and tried to say something, but it was not clear. I then asked her if she knew how much I loved her. She could barely put her thumb up enough to confirm that she did. Then I told her that there is someone who loves her more than I ever could. She was sort of baffled by this statement. I explained that Jesus loves you more than I ever could. "He will not leave your bedside or ever forsake you. He loves you so much that He laid down His life for you. He will redeem you and give you eternal life if you trust in Him as your Savior, and ask Him for the forgiveness of your sins." Even as I was sharing all of this with her, you could see it in her smile and the glow in her spirit. She did, in fact, know Christ as her personal Savior. The last picture I have of my mother and me was of both of our thumbs up. This was better than any movie critic's two thumbs up. It was the peace in my heart of knowing that my mom would spend eternity with God, and she would be free from this earthly body that had trapped her. God would set her free to her heavenly home three months later.

This story really highlights the importance of listening to people when you know God is speaking through them. He will tell you to act and go do something you know is the right thing to do. Being enrolled in college and taking time to leave and see her was not the easiest thing to do. I've confronted this with my own family and extended family. When God asks you to do something, you do it – even to the point of radical obedience. You may be asking yourself what does this mean or look like in my life?

Oftentimes, we live in a world where people place fake smiles on themselves and pretend like everything's okay. In our society, we are hesitant to show our vulnerability, our real struggles, and our issues. There is something to be said when another person shows a raw authenticity, but it can seem threatening or overwhelming. This transparency may make others uncomfortable. The fact is, we tend to cover things up or brush them aside, instead of talking about the deeper issues of the heart.

God asks us to confront sin. Be open and share your struggles and burdens with one another, while others may continue to avoid it. When we recite the Lord's Prayer: "Lead us not into temptation." We ask him to "deliver us from evil." We ask God to deliver us. During this period in my life, it seemed like temptation was around every corner - especially the temptation to avoid reconciliation. Yes, even the possibility of reconciliation with my own mother. This was when I was confronted by a friend who challenged that: "When was the last time you've seen your mom?" I said, "I'm not really sure. I'm sure she's seen me on TV – maybe watching my first football game."

My first game had come and gone, playing at Virginia Tech against New Jersey's Rutgers University. Deep down in my heart, I didn't think I had cared any more about seeing my mom. As they say, "Out of sight, out of mind." When you are confronted with doing the right thing, however, you have a choice. When

God gives us a choice, when asking Him about something, He gives us four possible responses. Yes, no, wait, or what most people usually do – take things into their own hands. And we know the outcome usually isn't good with the fourth option. In my case, I was choosing my own selfishness. Saying to myself "no." This is exactly where God would show His strength. He asks us to lay down our lives for Him. It's not about what we want, it's about what God would allow for His glory. He can use you if you will let Him. I remember a week later another friend saying, "Hey, I'll go with you."

At times people just need a friend to help bring things to fruition. God can use anyone! Yes, even you! Personally, my thoughts were, "Would it be better if I go by myself?" Ultimately, when a person doesn't have accountability, they usually divert responsibility to someone else. In this case, it was the responsibility of a person who considers themselves a Christian to take steps in reconciling, whether they were right or wrong. There are many ways people justify their actions, because they want to be right. In this case, and in many others, we should always take the first steps in asking for forgiveness. I'll never forget getting on that airplane, and thinking, "What am I going to say to my mother? How is this all going to unfold?" The answer is simple, God would give me not only the words to speak, but He would also help me to accept the forgiveness that I would receive later that day.

That thumbs up really meant more than I love you, and accepting Christ. It meant a love that restores and gives us freedom to let go and love. Love covers a multitude of sins, including our own. After leaving the hospital that day, I sort of knew that I may never see my mom again. When our hope is in the Lord, we can take great comfort and have peace in knowing that we will one day see our loved ones again who have died in Christ. After finding out that my mom had left to go be with the Lord, I was thankful to have my dad around to comfort me in this time of grief. I knew then I could trust in the Lord and not lean on my own understanding. Today, I am thankful for those who understand the importance of the ministry of reconciliation.

> You who were once far away from God.
> You were his enemies, separated from him
> by your evil thoughts and actions.
> Yet now he has reconciled you
> to himself through the death of
> Christ in his physical body. As a result,
> he has brought you into his own presence, and you
> are holy and blameless as you stand before him
> without a single fault.Colossians 1:21-22 (NLT)

CHAPTER SIX

Ten Trials of Troy, Five-Ten

Grandmother

Everybody's got a grandmother – some that everyone would want to be around, and others you try to stay clear of. Let's just say for the sake of protecting the innocent, my friend Joe never really liked being around his grandmother. Joe would intentionally avoid his grandmother at all costs, always concerned about being reprimanded or told what to do, in a sort of legalistic type of relationship. There were always expectations and strings attached, and a guilt trip that would come sooner or later. As for me all I can remember as a young boy, was that my grandmother really enjoyed video games (surprisingly). She always wanted to play Lee Trevino's Golf on the old Nintendo NES. It was very humbling to have your grandma beat you at any video game and especially at golf! I then learned where my competitive side came from. Not that winning a video game really matters, but in the end, it's more about spending time with people. A big part of our society today loves gaming. If a game brings people together then I am all for it.

Another part of the community we live in desires to earn people's approval. In fact, this is not only selfish, but leads to a deeper level of narcissism, which is something that I personally have had to battle, and others may struggle with this at times as well. Have you ever heard another person tell or say to someone, "You might want to quit smoking, because you could get emphysema"? No one ever thinks of these things when you are young. Growing up, most do not want to be told what to do or how to behave. Whether it is smoking cigarettes or anything else negative, people can just start a habit, and it sticks with you. Today some of these habits are leading our young people down a very broken road, specifically, when people start using any type of drug. There are going to be negative repercussions of some sort, whether they see them now or they surface later. When you think about what the Bible calls sin, it leads to death. Now smoking might not be a sin. However, some may classify or see it as sin if it is to the point of addiction. Some may say that smoking can take years off your life, that it smells bad, makes the individual more irritable when they do not smoke, etc. If a person exasperates another person, bugging them to quit, then chances are not likely that they will. Pray for them to stop if you really care for them.

Today there are many people who are living lies, and who are speeding up this process. Life is very fragile. At any moment, life can be taken away from us. Therefore, we have a responsibility to be good stewards of our time. Someone once asked how to spell the word love, and I read that it is spelled t-i- m-e. Please consider the time that you have been given. It is a blessing to be able to spend time with your children. It is a blessing to be able to spend time with your parents. Even the bad times are better than no time. I'm reminded of the blessings God gives us, including our grandparents and time spent with them. I'm reminded of the love that my grandfather had for my grandma. Love gives us the strength to live the life God intended for us.

When we help people, God sees this. Any one of us could

pass away tomorrow. As my lovely wife, Stacy, would say "just like that." "Do not be anxious about anything, but in everything by prayer and supplication with thanksgiving let your requests be made known to God." Philippians 4:6 (ESV). Oftentimes, people do just that – they pray for more time. Usually people at the end of their lives do not pray for more material possessions or finances but for more time to spend with those they love. For me having more time to spend with my Grandma getting to know her would have been wonderful, but the Lord took her home. When remembering a loved one who passed away, it makes you think. For me I thought of her being with God and it gave me the reality of knowing life is not forever on this Earth. We must give careful thought to the time we have with others. I am so thankful for the time that I had with my grandmother. Maybe, at this moment, the Lord is placing it on your heart to go and visit a loved one or a grandparent who may not be around much longer. Are you willing to sacrifice a little time and money for something that money cannot buy? Is now the time? Go.

Jack

This part of the book is written for those of you that have had great friendships over the years and you have lost them to suicide, like I mentioned earlier. My prayer is that this will give you hope and strength, knowing that sometimes people make decisions based on depression and circumstances. Let's start with the real Jack. I'll never forget first meeting Jack. I can say that I did not even want to hang out with him. He is the type of guy that tells you what you need to hear, not what you want to hear. You know a person you may be uncomfortable around, one who might say something that you do not want to hear at the time. Little did I know that God had a reason for Jack being such a big part of my life, and Jack allowed the Lord to use him in great ways. Are we willing to take the opportunity to allow God to use us? God can use us all if we allow Him. Jack once told me it brought him joy as he watched God change my heart. I recall my friend Dave saying the same thing.

When I was young in my faith, most of my prayers were self-centered or the ones that get you out of trouble when you know you have made a bad decision. Not that any of you reading have ever got in any trouble or have ever made any bad decisions. Like most people's best friends, I remember Jack for his willingness to stand by my side through ups and downs, through trials that he would later see come into my life. I remember his willingness to evangelize and share his heart and the hope that he had in Jesus Christ. He had a passion to help people grow in their walk with God. He was willing to walk through hardship and pain with some of his closest friends. He even used his passion for Virginia Tech football to open many opportunities to share about his faith and relationship with the Lord. Jack made such an impact on so many people. He had compassion and knew how to feed people. When he would invite people over, it usually involved some type of eating, whether it was a snack, dinner, or full-on Thanksgiving meal. Meals created an environment for fellowship. People would come together and share their hurts, but more importantly they would share how God was working in their lives. Jack had the hope of the Lord.

One specific story that I remember was the time he invited me on a hike to McAffee Knob in Virginia with some of the guys.

I was not prepared for this hike or the deep conversation that would develop when you hang out with a bunch of close friends. We talked about our future and our hearts' desires. I remember Jack specifically saying that our journey with the Lord was like going up and down the mountain, and that God was all around us when we were climbing up the mountain and when we were going down. That has really stuck with me over the years, because I always thought that God was someone we were trying to reach or attain to. I've come to find out that God is with us from the very beginning to the end. He is at the start of our life when we are at the base of the mountain and at the top. Sometimes this is a great illustration when you think of faith. It is this moment in time, where we give our life to God, that we have Faith. It seems to me that God, however, has been with us every step of the way, even before we accepted Him.

The next story would prove to be a very low point for me. I was on a mission trip with my friend, Tom, in Costa Rica. At that point in my life, I was asking God to really show and reveal Himself to me. He was doing that in so many ways, but it took me a little while to recognize. People echoed how God had used our short-term mission trip to help people. It seemed like everyone was on this "spiritual high," and that was when the call came in. All I remember was weeping on top of my friend's car as my friend, Ike, informed us of the news. Jack had probably taken his own life. The only comfort was knowing that he had put his trust and faith in Christ.

This does not, however, take away the pain of those left behind, when people make decisions to prematurely go to be with the Lord. God can use even the hurtful things in our lives to draw us closer to Him. When we go through pain, it opens our hearts to allow God to start healing us. People, however, can be on the opposite end of the spectrum where they close their heart to God and blame Him for the pain. God does allow us to go through hardship. As a matter of fact, the Bible is very clear that if we are truly following Christ we will go through pain, hardship, and suffering. At first I was in disbelief, and then I wondered if there was something that could have encouraged him in his walk with the Lord. Jack really liked Pepsi, and I am so thankful for God allowing us to share a few.

Lost season

When you are lost and walking away from God, you can be on a winning football team but still be losing as an individual. For so long my identity was in football, and unless God had taken my football career away, I would have never known it. My back injury led me to an understanding that there is a bigger battle we are fighting. Today and every day, we are in a battle for our families and friends. Praying for them is how we fight for them. The Bible talks about fighting the good fight of faith. On any given day we can only lean on God for our strength to fight another day in a world that seems to be full of disappointments, violence, and instability.

Growing up in Virginia Beach, my first introduction to football was when my dad had me play on a youth football league. I was only seven, but they put me with the older kids, because I was a lot bigger than most seven-year-olds. I did not like football at first. All the ten, eleven, and twelve-year olds were much bigger and stronger. All I remember was all the running we had to do, the up-downs, and endless hitting drills. I'm sure if you've played football you can relate and have thought to yourself, "Do I really want to play this game?" The next time I played football would be in middle school at Princess Anne. I remember all the kids I grew up with from the Pungo area, the countryside of Virginia Beach. What a great time we had. After practice, sometimes, we would all just get together and do ridiculous stuff. Those were the real bonding moments of my youth.

I can remember breaking a few rope swings in those days as well. They should have had weight-limit requirements posted on those things. I'll never forget my coach at the time saying, "Troy, you need to take it easy on your teammates during practice. This is your team. You save your real hard hits for the game." But I had always heard it said you play how you practice, and I always wanted to be a guy with a lot of tenacity. I always like to share a few embarrassing moments in life, and this one ranks pretty high up there. Although I liked to play football, I didn't know much about the game and the rules. Coach said that I would always stay in the game, and he said, "On offense, we have the ball. And on defense, you get the guy with the ball." Being that this was my first season playing football, I occasionally would not remember whether we were on offense or not, and when in doubt, I would go tackle the guy with the ball. Unfortunately, one time I tackled my teammate with the ball while on offense. So, after my middle school days of football came to an end, I went off to high school and played with several guys that would have college careers, including one who would end up in the NFL. High school football for me was an outlet for all the frustrations that I had at the time.

Dealing with life in my youth was not easy for me, especially knowing about my mom's sickness with ALS for about seven years, and our lack of a close relationship. There was always a temptation to do the wrong thing. Deep down, I knew that God had His hand on my life. I was too busy running away and trying to be the cool guy who played football. I also had too many girlfriends, which, coupled with football, occupied all my free time.

It is disappointing sharing this, but these things kind of go hand-in-hand with football. You have the party scene, girls, drugs, you name it. I thank God that He gave me such a great dad. He was there with a strong voice of reason and correction on many occasions when I was getting as he would call it, "A little too big for my britches." He kept me grounded, and I'm sure God kept Him grounded with all the prayers he had to pray for me. What a source of encouragement it is to have your parent or parents in your life. Be thankful even if you only have one. One is better than none I always say. My dad would say it's better to have one great parent than two bad ones. I completely agree! My dad is truly an example of what a man is, even though he has been overly gracious to me at times, or so my wife says. We all need to show grace when we make mistakes or say things we don't mean. Once my high school career ended, I was going through the college football recruitment process. What a time that was. It was great to see so many different universities, but most importantly, it was about finding a great education that would be provided for free.

Looking back, the cost of college was very unrealistic for me at the time, and I attribute the gift of a free education to God. He had given me the athleticism to play football, and this would provide a full scholarship, which I signed after visiting Virginia Tech. I became a Hokie – I'm still trying to figure out what a Hokie is, like the rest of the alumni. All I know is that we put up a great fight on the gridiron, and we reached for excellence. Thanks again Virginia Tech Coaching Staff for being great examples of men with integrity both on and off the field.

Once I was up at Virginia Tech, I just remember the horrific sound of the air horn waking us up for 6AM practices. This was my first taste of real work. I really respected my coaches, because they expected more of me than I expected of myself at times. And I would continue to push myself beyond my own personal limits. I'll never forget the words of one of my coaches at VT, "Troy, you are tougher than a 5-cent steak, son." I didn't know whether to laugh or just say, "Thanks coach." I went with the latter of the two. Going into the first season, it looked like they were going to red shirt me, which usually means they would not play me this year to save a year of eligibility. This didn't mean that I wasn't going to play in the first two games of the season, because back then you could play two games before the coaches made the final decision. The first game was against Rutgers, and just seeing all the fans in the stadium was sort of overwhelming. That's when I was reminded, with a nice slap on the helmet, "Get your head in the game. Not on all the people." College football is big business. It brings in revenue to universities. More importantly, however, it provides student-athletes with a great education, and in my case, a great outlet for all the hardships I had faced in life. It gave me a place to channel all my aggression and frustrations.

More importantly, it gave me a place to enjoy the camaraderie of a great bunch of guys – teammates – who fought for enough wins to make it to a national championship. Well, they say pride comes before the fall. For me it would be falling into a squat rack while trying to break another strength record for the VT football team. When you know you have an injury, you either keep pressing on, try to overlook it, or ignore the pain. Sometimes we need to take a good look at the reality of the situation. In this case, it was listening to the doctor and my coach. The question was "Do you want to walk when you are 40?" The natural answer is "yes" but for some, it is easier said than done. It was hard to hear for a person whose identity is football. In my case, I believe God took away my football career to open the door to greater things that He has planned for me. If your identity is in anything other than God, then you must understand that at any moment, it can be taken away for your own good. Things in life can unfold in ways that you may not have planned. Think about people you know.

Painful Past

Looking back over the years some can see that dealing with pain can be something they sort of get used to. For me it was a back injury that progressively got worse as the years went by. I loved baseball and swinging for the fence. Hitting home runs was where it's at. Then after putting down the bat and fully concentrating on football I noticed the constant pounding to my spine was catching up with me. One afternoon after winter workouts I recall my back hurting more than it usually did. We had our strength test coming up, and the first thing on my mind was breaking the squat record. Instead the weights broke me. Being in the weight room was always a blast. All of us pounded out the reps. Once I knew that my back was injured, I prayed that my back would feel better and that God would heal it. When I was in pain the only thing that seemed to help was prayer and relying on God to get me through it. It caused me to seek God more than I had before. This was true brokenness in a very literal way.

Car Accident

I was excited to head home early after exams from VT. It was starting to rain in the afternoon, and I was heading home a little faster than normal. This was when I started to notice the back tires of my car starting to slide out underneath me. The next thing I knew, I hit a pole, which I then bounced off and hit another pole head on. I got out of the car unscathed, and I remember saying, "Thank you God for your protection." After looking and seeing my car in total disrepair, I could only be thankful for His protection. The first police officer to the scene asked me if I was okay, and if I needed medical attention. I thought to myself, "No, I'm okay officer, but my car could use some medical attention." At this point in life, I took great care of this material possession called a car. I eventually learned that people are more important than cars! This accident would be the beginning of a breakthrough in my personal life. Nothing on Earth is more valuable than people. The love and time we spend with others can so often be taken for granted. I called my dad and told him that I had been in a serious accident. His first response, like any parent, was to ask if I was okay. I told him I was ok and that my shoulder hurt a little, but that was it. His next response was to ask what I was going to do to get back home. I told him I was going to get my car towed and find a way to get back home with a friend. I remember many rides from Tech to home. These were pivotal times.

Spending time on the road allows God to minister to you if you are desiring to hear His voice. The times I would listen to music during the drive and hearing the words of the songs would minister to me. Even though it was not Christian music "I Can Feel It in the Air Tonight" by Phil Collins, was one that seemed to minister to me in the strangest ways. I know that God's spirit starts to minister to a person long before they understand what a relationship with Christ means. Those nights on the road were therapeutic, dealing with the pain and trials in my past, and not knowing what God's plan was for my life or even my purpose. I think this is something everyone continues to learn. My wife Stacy would agree. She always says how she would really like God to paint a clear picture, and as we have both come to learn, God doesn't always make things so clear. He has a purpose in that too though, to get us to seek Him.

Katrina

As everyone remembers, this was one of the largest hurricanes that had ever hit the U.S. I remember, as it was approaching, the selfish attitude I had was to drive down to the Gulf Coast to surf. I thought this might be the best surf Texas had ever seen. Little did I know the devastation that I would be driving into during the days ahead or the phone call I would receive from a close friend named Chris. Chris called me and said, "Man, I know you were thinking about going surfing there, but this is about the time I was thinking about driving across country to move to California. Would you like to accompany me, and we could stop there and help one of those non-profit organizations to help with cleanup efforts?" I remember saying, "Sure, why not." It's amazing how

God will clear your schedule and provide you with time, so you can help with people whose lives have been turned upside down. Specifically, we ended up helping the people in St. Bernard's Parish who had been devastated by this massive storm.

Driving into the city of New Orleans was surreal. It was almost like I was watching a disturbing movie of what it would look like if there really were ghost towns. No cars were driving into the city, and we didn't see any cars coming out. Every now and then we would see a helicopter fly over, and once we got closer to the Ninth Ward, we saw a few military police and people directing us to where the volunteers were located. Seeing people walking around looking for their parents was heart wrenching, not to mention the lives that were lost and graves that were upturned. Seeing boats on the road and houses completely flattened, seeing churches with nothing but a few pews left standing, you almost had to think we were in some war zone. Well, the reality is that we are in a war zone. There is a war zone going on for our souls. The Bible says very clearly that the war is over our souls, and the enemy would love to convince us that following the Gospel is pointless. The only comfort the people had, however, was the love of God and the Holy Spirit which moved both Chris and I to help these people who were affected. Our deep sympathy went out to people, and the only hope we can have is in Christ.

It's amazing how a storm like that can bring great humility to a person. You couldn't look to your own interest anymore, it was really about the interest of others. We knew that we were all equal. God does not look at people with partiality. He sees us all the same. He loves all of us as His children. Even God sent His son Jesus, "Taking the form of a servant, being born in the likeness of men." Philippians 2:7 (ESV). For Chris and I, we were just being obedient. Some of the highlights of the trip for us were learning about what God's work really looked like, and doing things God's way for His glory. We will not forget the "meals ready to eat" that the military had provided us and looking at the container ships that the storm blew into the middle of the road. I guess that's the difference between where I used to be and where I am today. Much like the Apostle Paul, who said that the Gospel is shown in many ways and through the prayers of others. The Gospel shows the encouragement of God's grace, and we could come together side-by-side for God's faith to be seen while we loved people who were displaced, discouraged, and heartbroken. I'm glad I had a fellow worker named Chris along the journey and a few fellow soldiers joining in, laboring side-by-side with us as well. God says in His Word, that partnership means both giving and receiving. In the last few days that we were there, I remember journaling about the comforts and the luxuries that we have as people who live in the U.S. It truly showed me that wonderful things can be accomplished when people come together for the common good.

I remember telling Chris about an individual I met, but the story was about this individual and their spouse both looking for their yacht. I remember the individual openly said, "We have lost everything!" I walked over and replied, "You didn't lose everything. You still have your life and your family. Your vessel can be replaced." Life cannot be replaced, and it is very fragile. I may never know what the loss of a yacht is like, but I do know that the loss of a loved one can be devastating. At this point, I shared with this individual about the goodness of God and the hope we have in Him. Our hope cannot be in our material possessions.

If you have Jesus in your heart, then you have something that is priceless, and with the hope and strength that only the Lord can provide, you can make it through anything.

Romans 5:3-5 says: "And not only this, but we also exult in our tribulations, knowing that tribulation brings about perseverance; and perseverance, proven character; and proven character, hope; and hope does not disappoint, because the love of God has been poured out within our hearts through the Holy Spirit who was given to us" (ESV). I basically told this person that I pray that your hope is in God. Before I left, this person said thank you for encouraging me during this moment. The person went on to say, "This must be the result of God's work within you to be here doing this work, at this moment, in the middle of nowhere, just to encourage us in our most discouraged point in our life."

That's just the way God shows up in a person's life. We never know when or where we may be the conduit that God uses to help share the hope that everyone can have, even if they have lost everything.

Let's pause and think about conduit for a moment. Conduit carries something inside, usually wires that carry power. Power lights up the world. When you think about Christ, God sent His Son, Jesus, to give light to the world. When we have Christ in us, people can see this light.

Someone said, "Once you figure out that you can't figure God out, you've finally figured it out." God works in amazing ways! When you have faith, it can move mountains and even trees in our case. Towards the end of the trip, Chris and I were doing some work to remove trees from homes and driveways that were blocked. On this day, we spent some time with a woman who was getting up in age. She was sharing the details about the sound of the wind and the force of the water against the home while the storm raged outside. I remember asking her what took place. When you ask people, "Who do you pray to," you get some funny responses. The old saying, "You've never met an atheist in a foxhole" is very true. When people are desperate, they go to desperate measures, and in this case, I was desperate to see God work in the lives of those who felt neglected, abandoned, alone, hurt, and were uprooted by this storm.

Just the other day, I ran into a guy named Gary who shared his story about packing up all his stuff and his boat, then towing it up to the state of Virginia during Hurricane Katrina. He was saying, "Sometimes you just gotta listen to the Lord when he tells you to move." When Gary went back a month later to visit his friends, his whole block of homes where he once lived was gone. This correlates with the importance of listening to the Lord. If He is asking you or calling you somewhere, trust in His leading. Today, I believe many people get caught up in being content and comfortable where they are. God never says when we follow Him that it's about being comfortable. As a matter of fact, during this journey of life, we will all endure suffering in some way or another. Therefore, my prayer is that you would consider putting your trust and faith in the Lord, knowing that when you do come near to death, you can take comfort and know everlasting life awaits you.

The next thing you know, God showed us His sense of humor. Somebody threw a decent sized gecko on my head, and for some reason, I guess he didn't mind sitting there. A couple of pictures were taken, and a few people just started to laugh. God knew that's what we needed amongst all the labor that was done for the communities and how stressful being in this environment can be on you emotionally. It's funny how a gecko can get people to open up and talk. The group of us were talking about the beautiful colors and the way things change and how one moment a community can be so alive and the next minute be completely devastated and wiped away. God says that is exactly what happens in a person's heart. He wipes away our past when we give our life to Him. Some of our lives were very dark and were only colored with a lot of hurt and pain. The Bible says we are to no longer live in the past, and we are not slaves to sin. Now that we are free, we can live in the beauty of His grace and forgiveness. God gives us a future and a hope, and when we live for Him we are free from the slavery of sin. He gives us new life. He redeems us. A once broken, devastated place like our hearts is now one that is captivated by God's unconditional love and grace. It renews, restores, and redeems a person's life.

Oftentimes when people are affected in disturbing ways, it keeps them from moving forward. They almost get "stuck." The feeling of being trapped can be very overwhelming, and until you are released, it can be emotionally strenuous.

Back to Gary who was down in Louisiana, and God told him to pack up everything. He packed up his family, drove them and his boat to another state during Hurricane Katrina. His story is one of the importance of when God tells you to take steps to protect yourself and family, it is absolutely necessary to listen. In this case, it spared him and his family their lives. After hearing the firsthand account from Gary, he said, "How did you end up in this city here?" I said I wouldn't be here if it wasn't for the Lord. He said, "Nor would I be here either." That is what is so ironic. Thank God for grace.

CHAPTER SEVEN

The Story of a Ph.D. – Prayer, Hard Work, and Dedication

Well, if there's anybody in the world that was least likely to succeed, that would be me, especially according to my teachers. It was only by God's grace that I have attained any degree. According to my teachers in elementary and middle school, I was not only the least likely to succeed, but they also thought I had some problems. They said I would be lucky to make it out of high school. I can honestly say many of our children today probably have not succeeded due to the discouragement of teachers. On the other hand, many of our young people succeed when they are encouraged and asked to stay committed in their school endeavors.

Many people today become over achievers due to having a challenge in their life that they need to overcome. Many of our children come from broken homes and families. This is very difficult for young people, and they desire to feel accepted. They feel accepted when their parents and teachers reinforce their good grades, commitment, or behavior. In school, whether we like it or not, it becomes about performance. Thank God that it is not about our performance with Him. He loves us unconditionally.

It was only by Ph.D.: prayer, hard work, and dedication, that led me to completing this achievement in life. Many times, there were temptations to quit, give up, or just do something else. Some would say anyone could achieve this degree, but not many are disciplined enough to make the commitment for the years of education and study which is required to attain a degree of this level. Thanks and glory be to God, that when I wasn't always committed to Him, God stayed committed to me.

I'll never forget the day after I finished my master's program and my grandfather said, "What's next, a Ph.D.?" I told him, "No way. I'll never be smart enough to get a doctoral degree, granddad." Little did I know it's not about intellect, but it is about trusting God each step of the way.

I have learned over the years that even when you finish your doctoral degree, you still have a lot to learn. I have personally concluded, "I have now become smart enough to know that I'm not very smart." People today can make a lot of excuses as to why they can't do things, when in fact the Bible is clear, "I can do all things through Christ which strengtheneth me" Philippians 4:13 (KJV). Below is the insert of the acknowledgements page of my dissertation which gives honor to those I am thankful for during this journey called life. When working on this dissertation, it occurred to me that without God, and His abundant Grace, this degree would not have been attainable. Therefore, it only seems appropriate to give the glory and honor to God which can be seen in the last line, which is the whole reason the Lord gave me the strength to finish the degree in the first place. To God be the glory!

Acknowledgements

Without the support of many people, this dissertation would not have been possible. First, I must recognize my Lord and Savior Jesus Christ for his guidance along this journey. For those of you who would like to know, my definition of the acronym for Ph.D. is prayer, hard work, and dedication. Second, I would like to thank my dad, Scott S. Smith, for encouraging me to excel when it seemed impossible and for constantly supporting me each step of the way. You have truly gone far and beyond what it takes to be a wonderful dad and friend!

The next group of people I would like to thank is my committee members. To my committee chair, Dr. Rich Stratton, thank you for kindly guiding me and helping me to understand the importance of independent research and the value of knowledge. My committee: Dr. Michael Herndon, thank you for your intercession, encouragement, and friendship along the way. Dr. Kerry Redican, thanks for your willingness to give your valuable time, guidance, and prayer to this dissertation. Dr. Billie Lepczyk, thank you for your constructive suggestions throughout the research process.

Finally, I have to recognize and thank my family for remembering me in their prayers. Thanks for all your support and love! Special thanks to my grandfather, Norman D. Smith, for his inspiration, encouragement, and for imparting the significance for me to undertake and complete this Ph.D.. Thanks to all of my friends and cohorts who gave me direction, support, encouragement, endless editing efforts, and for believing in my ability to complete this degree.

In closing, I want to honor the Father, the Son, and the Holy Spirit for making me all that I am today. May I continue to do all things for His Glory!

(Note: I would now change the above "my ability" to "His ability through me.) It was His ability through me. Look at the Greek word Dunamis, which means strength, power, and ability. It was not ever about my power, might, or strength. Only God's alone.

I know that God really expresses his immeasurable grace right when we get to the point of surrender, because it's when we are weak, He is strong. It allows us to give up our independence and become dependent on God. For me at this point in my life, I had to surrender a lot of things. I could not lean on my own understanding, but I had to trust God taking me through this process. When a person starts a project or makes a commitment, we must believe that God brings all things to completion. I experienced this firsthand while watching my best friend complete their law degree. Everyone handles things differently. Watching a friend battle with anxiety, frustration, anger, and doubt can be very difficult. When we see people go through these types of emotions, this should draw us to God by praying for them and letting them know they are not alone through these challenges.

About a week before graduation, I recall the Lord clearly

putting two pieces of Scripture on my heart: Romans 10:9 and Romans 12:12.

> "If you confess with your mouth that Jesus is Lord and believe in your heart that God raised Him from the dead, you will be saved" Romans 10:9 (NLT)

> "Rejoicing in hope, persevering in tribulation, devoted to prayer," Romans 12:12 (NASB)

These verses were taped to my graduation cap for any onlookers to see that it wasn't about me, but about God and His Truth. Talk about looking foolish – but one older gentleman in the crowd was so encouraged by the cap, that he prayed that someone would come to a knowledge of salvation out of all the thousands of people in attendance.

When a person finally gets to the point of "I can't," God steps in and reminds us of the word "can." God can do all things! He is the author and finisher of faith and even dissertations.

CHAPTER EIGHT

Blessed is the Man Who Finds a Wife – The Love Story

It was a cool fall evening, and I was spending it with a great friend of mine. We headed out to a place that we could not find on our own, but when God wants you to be at a certain place at a certain moment, He will get you there. Thank God for GPS! This is what I call God's Positioning System. This would be an evening that will not be forgotten. This was the night that I first laid eyes on my beautiful wife to be.

The night started out with me getting in the way of myself. I had asked my friend, Roger, if we could leave. I thought to myself, "Why did we come to this Christian get-together in the first place?" I felt awkward, isolated, and alone as many Christians do during those times. After Roger wandered off (as he usually does) I found myself looking at a bunch of faces I didn't know. But as you'll learn about me, I have never met a stranger. My usual routine is to always leave a place with new friends. I really do believe Jesus is great at making people feel loved and accepted. This has also been something very intentional in my personal life. That night, even though I had come there feeling alone, I left knowing a wonderful woman named Stacy. I would later find out that she would indeed be the woman God had picked out for me. Stacy already knew.

Do you want me to just keep going here? Well, of course you do! This chapter is the love story. Well, you could say she made me smile. She even made me laugh a lot. She was a driven woman who was pursuing a law degree, and this was also attractive. After much prayer and talking to some other people about pursuing Stacy, the Lord had given me peace. When the Lord is behind something, He will align it with His perfect will and make things very clear. Have you ever prayed for confirmation? In my case, the Lord made things absolutely certain that she was the one.

Our first date – one of high class. We got a group of people together since I didn't like hanging out with women alone – a tremendous change from the college days. I purposefully did this to guard her heart and get to know her in a group first. I wanted to respect her and be a gentleman. Still, I failed her in many ways. For our first date, we went to a graveyard. Yes, you read this correctly. A graveyard. I picked her up somewhat early because I knew an adventure laid ahead. We headed down the road and got to know each other's likes and dislikes, along with some of our pet peeves. As we began opening up to each other, she got to hear me share a few wounds from my past. It was great to be able to share and not be judged. She was such an encouragement to me. I loved just looking at her lovely smile – and still do each day that we are married. We finally arrived downtown at an old church with a very old graveyard on the side of it. We started to talk about the importance of serving the Lord and trusting Him with the details of our lives.

You know a good woman when she brings you out on a date to a high-class restaurant like fast food. This night would be where we would have what some would call a DTR: define the relationship moment; for those who do not know the acronym, and yes, I may just be talking to the men here. Well, I guess when you think about it, every person has their own perspective. Personally, my view of a relationship looked more like a courtship. I was very intentional about pursuing this lovely lady, who today I can happily say is my lovely bride.

Having a wife like Stacy is such a inspiration, until she made me go camping in July. Let me tell you! It was hot and humid, and with a newborn, it really stretched us both. We can both look back and laugh now. One thing you quickly learn when you have a newborn is that you cannot do what you want to do. This is also learned by most people in the first week of marriage. Add a kid to the mix and you then begin to understand the term sacrifice. Ultimately, this means that both people in the marriage make decisions together, and it is not one sided. Joint decision-making starts with healthy communication. God will sometimes put a person in your life that you would least likely expect. I did not expect to marry up so high. God knew not only the desires of my heart, but He also considered the weaknesses that I personally have. God completes us, and He uses us to encourage one another when we need it most. A true blessing in any marriage is when you can accept each other's weaknesses while at the same time, reassuring one another in each other's strengths. In our marriage, the strength and foundation of our marriage is built on Christ, Who is the center of our relationship.

For most men, it seems like we have a lot of thoughts and plans, and praise God that He directs our footsteps. He led me right to Stacy and she is certainly included in making some of the biggest decisions we have made over the years. In a marriage, we are called to love our wives as Christ loves the Church. Today, hopefully, we can encourage and motivate one another to become more engaged in our marriage and passionate about our faith as we walk in the Lord. We need to be very intentional about being thoughtful. Sometimes being thoughtful does not happen naturally. Thank God for when it happens supernaturally. Think about a moment when you have been excited about something and you had a desire to share something. My desire was to be able to share our lives together and being able to give glory to God while surrendering to His leadership. Today the Lord still leads us!

Sometimes God will allow accidents to happen. Early in my dating relationship with Stacy, we had an opportunity to go to a ski resort, and I had a great time with her. I questioned whether I was the man to lead this woman, and deep down I can honestly tell you that I didn't know if I really was. On that trip, I was going to take a break from our relationship, but God had another plan. It would be the last run of the day (only our second), and I know God's Word says pride comes before the fall, but in Stacy's case it was speed that came before the fall.

Wow, she could really go fast down the mountain. We were both bombing the hill, and before I knew it, I looked over and saw Stacy hit an ice patch. It was a traumatic fall, and I remember thinking she might be dead. At this point, I took my snowboard off and walked over to her and asked, "Stacy, are you okay?" She didn't respond right away, and I prayed that she was okay. I even said, "Lord, I pray she didn't break anything." But I guess that prayer only covered bones, because we found out later that week that she had torn her ACL. It was during this trip that I fell in love with my wife to be. Her injury gave me the opportunity as a man to be sensitive and compassionate. I remember just how strong she was. She didn't even really cry until I compared her to another woman that had the same injury, and she said, "What about me? Don't you care about me?" I said, "Yes, of course, let me go for help."

I flagged someone down and the next thing you know, there was a little wrapped up Stacy, who looked like a yellow burrito, headed down the slope in a little yellow bag. We got to the lodge where they assessed her injury, and her knee was as big as mine. That's pretty big to say the least. We knew there was obviously something wrong, so like any man, I decided to take her on a road trip to VT. Little did Stacy know, it was about 4 hours out of the way, and not on the way home at all. As I showed her around where I grew up, she did enjoy seeing the campus and the stadium that I played football in and what most would call, "My old stomping grounds." We started to head home around 4 in the afternoon.

This would lead to the next exciting part of our adventure. Heading through the mountains was very peaceful for both of us. We enjoyed our conversation, even though our relationship was just beginning at this point. The next thing you know, a rock flew up and busted the windshield of my truck. It was just sort of one of those days when life unfolds. After about another 100 miles down the road, the truck engine shut down. We pulled over but it wouldn't start. It wouldn't turn over, nothing. God had a plan in all of this. We were on the side of the road, might I add, it was very dark, and I thought "Lord, could you please help us in this situation?" That was when we both witnessed the blue lights behind us. A state trooper asked what was going on, and I explained to him that I had no idea. Deep down thinking to myself that the float in the fuel tank has been sticking every once in a while, after it falls under a half a tank. We thought that the truck could have run out of fuel, so he offered to give me ride to get some fuel. This was very humbling, because the gauge still read over a quarter tank. I explained to him that the young lady in the back of the truck had a bad knee injury, and he asked whether she would mind staying there by herself. I was thankful she had a gun with her for protection, so I went with him. We came back, put the fuel in and realized we were still stranded, because the truck still wouldn't start even after priming it. Then I made the phone call to a local towing company to get us the next 100 miles home. It was a long 100 miles home in the small cab of the tow truck with Stacy's foot propped up in the air on the dashboard, and I was sitting sideways between the tow truck driver and her. I looked over about an hour into the trip as this driver was falling asleep at the wheel. I gave him a gentle nudge, and asked him, "Hey, tell me what is your story." He continued to talk the rest of the way home. What a long day and night. You know you truly love someone when you're willing to lay down your life and sacrifice for them. With Stacy, at this point, there was no one to take care of her. She was the damsel in distress. I remember having to carry her from car to car, up and down flights of stairs. I think she started to fall more in love with me at this point. Come to find out that the dealership never did find anything wrong with the truck. They said it started right up when they looked at it. Maybe God wanted us to spend some more time together.

She knew I was willing to put everything else aside to help care for her. Which leads me to sharing a Scripture that we both hold dear to our hearts this very day. Before she went under for surgery, I prayed over her, and asked God that she would, "Be anxious for nothing but through prayer and supplication ... letting her request be known before God." Philippians 4:6 (ESV). I asked for a complete recovery and that the surgery would go well. When she woke up from the anesthesia, she was a little overwhelmed, and kept asking me where in the Bible the verse "God will give you the peace that passes all understanding." Philippians 4:7 (ESV). This verse was the next verse after the one we prayed before she went into surgery. God's Word says He is the beginning and the end, the author and finisher of our faith. "And we know that God causes all things to work together for good to those who love God, to those who are called according to His purpose" Romans 8:28 (NASB). I knew God was working out our relationship to give Him glory and honor for His purpose.

CHAPTER NINE

Season of Love and Love that Lasts!

When a man finds a woman, he is blessed indeed! This chapter explains how a man becomes a sacrificial man. When I met Stacy, she was a woman who I knew loved God. This was what initially attracted me to her. The Lord put it on my heart to ask her what she feared one day and if she said the Lord then I would marry this woman. Sure enough she said, "I fear the Lord." I was, however, not fully convinced I was supposed to get married but just needed to trust God. God has a funny sense of humor. Stacy was finishing her last year of law school at the time and I was finishing up my Doctoral degree from Virginia Tech. Little did I know, after trying to set her up with a few people who would later be in our wedding party, one of my friends revealed she was smitten with me. Valentine's Day seems to be a holiday that sneaks up on us each year, and I can only reflect on what an amazing love we share, not just on the holiday, but 365 days a year!

It is ultimately the Love of God that we see in one another that holds our marriage together. Stacy reminds me that a couple that prays together stays together! Statistics even give validity to this! When you come to the end of yourself and depend on God, then you're at the point where you can truly love someone. Stacy and I pray together – a lot! This helps immensely during the tough times in life and ministry. It is a love that only God could put together. When I go to a card store for a special occasion I am reminded just how much a simple expression of love can have such a great return in our marriage. Flowers would be just as nice, but most of the time she would prefer dark chocolate!

Some say marriage is made in Heaven. I truly agree with this. A marriage flourishes with love, respect, patience, kindness, gentleness, and not keeping a record of wrongs. These are some of the fruit of the Spirit and the last one in 1 Corinthians 13 can be difficult for a lot of people. These are not a list of things that I could have come up with, but they are a list that only a Loving God and Creator of marriage could come up with. Love takes pleasure in the truth and always protects, trusts, and hopes! Did I mention it perseveres as well? This is a list that is very dear to my heart, as it is to Stacy's, which comes from 1 Corinthians 13:1-13.

We both understand that without Christ as the center of our marriage, our marriage would not be possible. After taking some time to reflect over the years of our marriage, we can both take great comfort in knowing that God is the one who arranged our marriage. Not all marriages last, and today the statistical reality suggests that if you do not love one another sacrificially, it cannot last. Some people's marriages are made on emotional whims and out of wanting a relationship to work out. I have heard two great pieces of advice from very wise people: do not awaken love before its time – much like Song of Solomon 8:4, and it is always good to wait on the Lord. Allowing God to arrange your marriage is the best decision a person can make. God does not make mistakes, but we do. The Lord above all, knew exactly what was best for Stacy and me. This included God being the foundation of our marriage and our making a covenant before Him.

What about Baggage?

Stacy and I reminisce by looking back at our wedding congregational song and singing: "Worthy is the Lamb who was slain. Holy, Holy, is He," which is from "Revelation Song" by Jennie Lee Riddle. My wife and I both carried some baggage of our past into our marriage, just like all people do. Mine was packed full, probably well over the fifty-pound limit. Thank God, He asked me not to pack for this trip. Stacy packed very lightly, maybe just her Bible before we met, even though my baggage was over the required limit she said to me that God made me new, and there are no weight limits with the Lord. We can both agree that we have different outlooks on life and different preferred temperatures both inside and outside the house. At times, we know that logic defies even us being together, and we are reminded that God alone is the one who has brought us together.

Oftentimes we take a lot of baggage through this life that we were never intended to carry. Most people think of luggage and baggage when they take a trip for a vacation. I believe Jesus is asking us to just leave our luggage or baggage behind and start a permanent vacation in His Grace. I know for me, my back can really start to hurt, my feet ache, and I get tired when I carry around unnecessary baggage or what some would call excess junk from the past.

A lot of people today have emotional luggage that holds them down. Some of this luggage includes, but is not limited to, worry, disappointment, fear, guilt, shame, and the list goes on. No wonder people get so weary these days, and then you add the evening news to that and it's a recipe for disaster. There's not much hope in the evening news unless they are covering a story about how God used another person to share the Gospel of Salvation in a hopeless world. Hopefully, this encourages you to give your burdens to the God-man called Jesus, the Good Shepherd. He is greater than any problem, stress, or worry you could ever have in your life. God hears us when we pray to Him. He is the love of our life and the power that picks us up when we're down. When a person has Christ in his or her life they know that the Holy Spirit is within, giving them a future and a hope for the road ahead. Where does the road lead?

Ultimately, this destination is a permanent vacation in heaven, if you will, of eternal life with Jesus. When you have the Good Shepherd, you have enough grace for every sin and enough guidance for every turn you make in life. You have adequate light for every dark area that life can have, and rest assured He gives you the strength for each storm you will go through. When you take a vacation with Christ, you have everything you need. In this book you have read about people who have had cancer, faced tragic storms in their lives, have lost their homes and loved ones. However, when tragedy strikes, which it will, our hope and trust can only be in Christ. Some people often ask why is life worth living, and we can respond by sharing the gospel and our faith with others to give them the same hope we have. People may come to you and say they have lost everything. Hopefully your response will be, "Have you lost your faith, loved ones, and salvation?" If their response is no, then they haven't lost anything that matters in eternity. These are the things that matter most, but society tends to focus so much on materialism and how many commodities we have. We can oftentimes lose our focus or our determination and just want to give up.

Think about the words of Paul for a moment. One of my wife's favorite verses when I am growing weary is 1 Timothy 6:6, which simply states, "Godliness with contentment is great gain" (NIV). Often, we become discontent, and it's usually because of something we desire to gain. Our contentment must come from Christ, and hopefully we understand how precious having Christ is in our life. God's Word clearly says that He will give you rest from your burdens, when you feel weary and overwhelmed. I've heard it said that worry, anger, and bitterness are all like acid because acid destroys its own container. We can sometimes hold on to things like worry and the worry inside of us starts to deteriorate our bodies in the form of health issues.

Anxiety goes hand-in-hand with worry, but when we trust in Jesus he meets all our needs. What a different life we can live when we allow God to lead us! When we ask God for discernment to go the right way or to do the right thing it's about learning to trust Him and in His timing. The results can be amazing! When God's hand is operating in our lives we are not distracted by all the cares of this world. I like to remind people to meet today's problems with Christ's strength. So often we can relive yesterday's problems which are over and gone. Other times we live in the worry about the future and its problems which have not yet come, but God gives us strength and hope for today. Jesus makes a lot of similar points in Matthew 6:34. He states, "Don't worry about tomorrow, because tomorrow will have its own worries. Each day has enough trouble of its own" (HCSB). The simple way to remind ourselves of some of our burdens is to get out of the way. I know first-hand we can get in our own way at times. God does not like human pride, arrogance, or self-righteousness. God desires us to get over ourselves, because it's not about us. When we make a good self-assessment, we can all honestly admit that we have made mistakes. Remind yourself not to take success too seriously. Walk humbly before God. Having those you love around you can help you have a good assessment, and God can use them to help you grow in your relationship with Christ.

The most amazing thing, when you think about it, is when we will be welcomed home in heaven. God's Word says that "He will wipe away every tear from [your] eye," Revelation 21:4). One day we will dwell in the House of the Lord forever. God's Word says our body must die so that our new body can live. God's goodness is so wonderful. He gives mercy to forgive every sin. God is such a great Father. God does not always give us what we want, but rather a good father gives a child what is needed.

God's Word also talks about healing the brokenhearted in Psalm 147:3. Think of the words that Jesus shared in the New Testament:

"I am the Good Shepherd. The Good Shepherd
sacrifices His life for the sheep." John 10:11 (NLT)

When you think about sheep, sometimes they can go astray, they get stuck, and are much like all of us who are vulnerable to aging, sickness, and loss. When you think about the words of people in the Bible who had wounded hearts and you think about God's Word, you realize God's Word brings healing and hope. He repairs the holes in our heart. Just imagine if your heart were to look like a piece of swiss cheese, then God turns you into a beautiful whole piece of mozzarella. Pretty cheesy analogy, I know, yet beautiful.

Loneliness can often be God's way of getting our attention. God never intended for us to go through this journey of life alone. He walks through life one step at a time with us.

Can you love someone when they do not love you back? God does this, and we are to model this in our marriages. True love is this: when we love without expectation and would still love another person even when they do not return that love back to you. God works all things out for His glory. He first started by drawing us to Himself and then together. He is the cement that holds our marriage together. The Bible states very clearly in 1 Corinthians 13:8 "Love never fails" (NIV). Unfailing love is sustained by a gracious God who expresses His love through each of us. Only God's love is consistent and constant. May we be reminded that the only way a marriage can last is by complete and total dependence on God.

God made us to experience love because God is the source of love and can fill our need for love as no other person or thing can. God showed His love by giving the ultimate sacrifice, so we could have eternal life. It's not that we loved God first, but that He first loved us (1 John 4:19). We can all use this as a model for loving one another. He took away all our sins. If God loves us that much, His love can overflow from us to love one another fervently. LOVE IS PATIENT! In the Scripture one thing it says, love never gives up! Love is always hopeful and endures through every circumstance. Let someone know you love them today!

Now we come to this word called forgiveness. If you love someone, you forgive them, no matter how deep the stain of his or her sins or how bad you think the situation is. God can fix and remove the past when we allow Him. He makes all things new, and He cleans us all as beautiful as freshly fallen snow.

> Come, let us discuss this," says the LORD."
> Though your sins are like scarlet, they will be as
> white as snow; though they are as red as crimson,
> they will be like wool." Isaiah 1:18 (HCSB)

Notice the "all" in the following verse. "If we confess our sins, he is faithful and just to forgive us our sins and to cleanse us from all unrighteousness." 1 John 1:9 (NLT)

CHAPTER TEN

The Importance of
Community and Family

Every community has a name to their fellowship. The Bible calls this the Body of Christ. Hopefully, every family has a meaning to their name. Ours is written out below. Clarity helps with our mission in life, along with clarifying questions. Someone once said, "What does the name Smith mean or stand for?" I replied, "I guess like a coppersmith." Think about metal. It is usually molded into something. God shapes us every day if we allow Him. This is how God intends it to be. That's how metal takes its form. Iron sharpens iron. We came up with "What it means to be a Smith" about seven years ago. We all have significance, and our significance comes from God. In our family, we like to say we have a central theme or core values.

Core values as a Smith family member

- Love Jesus
- Live out our Faith
- Be loving, compassionate, and gracious
- Respect others
- Set personal boundaries
- Discern with the wisdom God gives us
- Tell the Truth

It's just that simple. Just as we were typing, our daughter learned the importance of sharing, and this is something God has done for each of us by sending His Son Jesus. He has offered and shared eternal life with us. Having what some would call building blocks – or in some people's case stumbling blocks. They stumble through life and never learn to build their lives around Christ. Today's society seems to build upon things that have no eternal purpose or value. We enjoy seeing our daughter building on the principles of God's Word – not just a family name, but on the Name above all names.

In the last year God has taught me so much about the importance of family, especially when you lose a child or someone close to you in your family, like a parent. In the beginning chapter of Genesis, God talks about community and family. The Father, Son, and Holy Spirit, all three in one. This brings us to a place where God desires to meet you. The Holy Spirit is very mysterious, and no one knows what He is doing. I love the word "omnipresence" – God being present everywhere, all the time. He is here among us, around us, at any moment, at any time and in any place. During the writing of this book we experienced one of the toughest things for a parent to hear.

"The heartbeat of your child has stopped."

When you first hear these words, you do not believe what you hear. Then you walk through the pain of losing a child. You ask yourselves a lot of questions at first. Or the what ifs. Then God reminds you that He is a loving, caring, gracious God. He can heal our hearts in any circumstance when we allow Him. Today Stacy and I can have peace knowing that our baby

Nazareth Simeon Smith is now with the Lord and my mom Carolyn Lee. Our daughter sat with me at the table and she said: "Yes dad, Nazareth is with my other Grandma in heaven." Today be thankful for what you have and everyone you have in your life. If you have one child think of those who cannot have children. If you have feet be thankful for the feet God has given you. Some people do not have feet. Take time to remember those who God has placed in your life. Just look at your children for a moment and gaze on the wonder of His beautiful creation.

Well, some things aren't very clear until you get a good story to illustrate, so I will share.

Some men maybe wonder whether they should get married. A pastor once asked me, "Well, do you still want to have sex? And if the answer is yes, then you need to get married." I know a lot of people, within the sexually saturated society we live in, really need help with this. Help starts with God and asking Him to give you self-control. Some people jump into what I would call pre-fab or already made families, by marrying someone with children, some may have a parent or spouse pass away and they re-marry. Some bump into someone, hook up, and then they have a child. Yes, you can probably figure out what this means. They meet someone any old way and give themselves to them willingly, foolishly, immorally. I know for myself, God really has a sense of humor. I would run into my future wife on several occasions, not knowing that this would be the wonderful woman that God would bless me with. Let's just say I had this friend that's very close to me, and he said, "That's your future wife, Troy." I said in response, "No way, not a chance!" Well, while visiting California I would end up running into her three thousand miles away from where we both lived. She was finishing up a professional degree, as I was, and so I'm sure the last things on our minds was getting married. Little did I know, it was on her mind. As for me, I was in the bachelor for life club, so I'll fill you in here as my wife will say.

Troy thought he was going to be a bachelor for life, but God had other plans for him. Troy was waiting on the Lord and on the right person. The whole first year that I had casually met Troy, I was really struggling with still being single at my age. I had never had a serious boyfriend and thought God was holding out on me. I was struggling with God and even miffed at Him, but I kept talking it out with Him and finally realized that I had to trust God with this area of my life too. I had to come to terms with being okay not ever being married if that was what God had for me. Once I surrendered it to God, He graciously put us in one another's lives. That's something that's cool about our story, we were both okay with not being sure of ever being married, and God worked it all out!

Yes, He did indeed! Amen.

CHAPTER ELEVEN

The Privilege of Prison,
the Story of Mario;
and that Day

There was a great game back in the '90s that everyone seemed to enjoy. It has had a lasting impression on most gamers, including myself. Most would not consider me a gamer, but I remember one year of my life spending an incredible amount of time on a very well-known game called Mario Brothers. Looking back, my time could have been better spent, but I was hooked on playing this game. Maybe all that time wasn't wasted after all, considering the following. I can draw wisdom from it now. When you think of the Mario Brothers game, it's a lot like a person's journey in their faith. Ok, you are wondering where this is all going but stay with me. All I know is in the beginning of the game, much like being born again, we must start somewhere. Much like our journey in Faith. We start by turning on the power button to the gaming system. This is the first thing we need: Power. Power is given from God. This is where I would like to say the Holy Spirit moves in our life. The Lord empowers us. Then we see the beginning of the game, much like when we are 'baby' Christians or young in our faith as followers in Christ. So, let me explain the game as it relates to trusting in Christ. Here we go.

Doo-doo-doo-da-do DOOT!

We start out small like Mario, walking along, then we start looking around knocking on things, opening doors and it's kind of like God knocking on our hearts. We don't know what's behind the door and in some cases, we pass the door, totally ignoring it. In the case of the game door, sometimes you get advanced to other places. In the Lord, He advances us in life, and we're not always sure of the meaning. Then, in the game, we look around and find an item that allows us to grow and get bigger. This represents us maturing in our Faith. Next, we find an item called a star as we continue down the path, which makes us invincible to the enemies' attacks. The star is like the Holy Spirit, who is protecting us from harm and danger caused by Satan or other demonic forces. Once you find this other weapon – firepower – it's much like the sword of the Spirit, which is our Bible. When we engage in reading and memorizing Scripture, we fight the enemy with the Word of God and with prayer.

Now the game always seems to look easy to some people. Key emphasis on "seems to look easy." You can shoot those fireballs so far away, and you can always maintain a safe distance from the enemies. Think about creating safe distances from something that can hurt you spiritually.

What I've noticed about temptation in my personal life is that it is always right around the corner, and sometimes it just sneaks up on you like the enemies in the Mario game. This is why we need other protection and accountability. It helps us to know that the Holy Spirit lives in us, and when the enemy does attack us, we may lose power, get knocked down (in the game we become small) or regress, but we don't die. Sometimes the attacks will make us smaller in our faith, but there is always opportunity to grow in our faith because of this wonderful thing called Grace.

Biblically, it is the unmerited favor of God. It's like having the code where you can have unlimited lives in the game. You unlock the game. God gives us grace to unlock our lives. God gives us an unlimited amount grace, and when we come to the end of this life, we have an eternal life. Our eternal life starts when we accept Jesus Christ into our hearts as our Lord and Savior, which is His gift to us by His grace! He redeems us from sin. I guess you could say the lava is like the fiery pit of hell, and with God's protection, like in Mario Brothers 3, you can jump in the lava, swim under fire and lava, yet never get burned. When we finally get to the end, we see God defeat the enemy. When we give our life to Christ He gives us eternal life and unconditional love. The enemy has been crushed and defeated, then He receives us, the bride, like we receive the princess at the end of the game.

Everybody desires the freedom from bondage, brokenness, and despair, just like those who are incarcerated. They are those who are often forgotten unless you know of someone in prison. These prisoners are not the only ones who are incarcerated. Some people can be incarcerated in their own hearts. In the life God has given me, it has been a great privilege to visit those who are in our jails. So often, people in prison are forgotten, but God sets us free in our hearts to love.

One person that I have enjoyed making friends with is serving a (LWOP) life without parole sentence. This individual shot 5 people and killed 3. Someone told me their sentencing was something like 1,558 years. Unless God intervenes, then this is where this person will spend the rest of their earthly life. When a person is facing life in prison without parole, this may be more punishment and difficult to deal with than anything. It would be harder for some than the death penalty. So often we think removing people from society is the answer, and others would say to introduce them to Christ, who can restore them spiritually, emotionally, and physically while being in prison.

It's amazing to think that people who are in prison write letters to encourage people on the outside, as this person has done for me and our family over the last years. This is exactly what the Apostle Paul did when he wrote his letter of encouragement to the church of Philippi. Paul was in jail and the book of Philippians is one of my favorite books in the Bible no matter where it was written. My wife Stacy and I even share one of our favorite Scripture verses in Philippians 4:6-7 as mentioned earlier with her ACL knee surgery.

> Do not be anxious about anything, but in everything by prayer and supplication with thanksgiving let your requests be made known to God. And the peace of God, which surpasses all understanding, will guard your hearts and your minds in Christ Jesus. (ESV)

Norman wrote, "If there is anyone in church that could use a shot of hope, some inspiration, or maybe is having a tough time with gratitude, feel free to let them know I would like to encourage them." This individual wrote a letter to our church that was shared one Sunday morning. I said, "I guess the topic of the letter could be perspective on the inside of the prison walls." Some would say the justice system has catastrophically failed. We have a system set up where you wear a jumpsuit that feels like a uniform of shame and disgrace. Prisoners are required to wear the outfit as a constant reminder of their crime. God states that we are forgiven. He does not see our past mistakes or crimes, whether guilty or not. There are, however, earthly consequence to all our actions.

The whole point here is that we all have valid concerns, especially when we look at fixing a very broken system. There is one individual that I took the time to interview, and he let me know he has now spent over 16 years of his life locked away. What is most disheartening though is that we don't understand how or why people become repeat criminal offenders. He said, "When looking around the cells I saw these men who are lost, but they don't even know they're lost or how to begin a changed life, so how can they ever be found?" He always believed the punishment of doing the crime would be enough of a deterrent for him to not commit the crime in the first place. He thought the time of being behind bars for so long would help keep him from going back – especially making the same mistakes. He says the recidivism rate is so high in this country because most people do not know when to admit they have a deeper problem. This inmate stated they had to come to a place where they recognized they had a spiritual malady; their change had to start from the inside out.

The definition of hopelessness is defined in a drug addict's terms as:

"When you really think about drug addiction you have got to believe that someone who would put themselves through what we drug addicts do, has to suffer from some degree of hopelessness. Some describe it as a feeling that everything is not going to be alright."

For this person's story they stated that there is a very real physical feeling, an ache of desperation. He once looked up the word desperation and it was defined as "recklessness due to despair" and that defined him. It also defines a lot of the people who continue to break the law to obtain something that they feel makes everything alright again. He mentions money, drugs, sex, and the list goes on, but ultimately concluding there is a spiritual problem. He used to believe there was something that would make him feel whole and complete apart from God, but he realized this is not possible. I have never heard of a jail or prison that offers an environment conducive to diagnosing and treating a broken spirit. Most of the prisoners, however, end up here because of this brokenness. The only medicine for these diseases is LOVE, kindness, compassion, and forgiveness. Prisons are very cold, dark, desperate and lonely places, and apart from Christ, there is no hope for these incarcerated.

I can tell you from my firsthand experiences of visiting these inmates, this brokenness is very real. Oftentimes when I see repeat offenders, I see their spiritual condition worsens. There is an increase in hate, anger, fear, all the elements that lead to lies and destroys the core of who they are. Inmates I know often ask themselves, "What brought me here?" And they look at the environment they are in, and some think the system is supposed to help them change. The reality is, the only person who can change us is God. The power of the Holy Spirit in us can change us. He changes us when we surrender and allow Him. It seems to me, at this point, when a person believes in God He starts the restoration process in our lives. When we allow Him to come into our heart, we are asking him to fix the problems deep within us, which is sin and our past mistakes. When we allow Him to increase and ourselves to decrease, this allows us to reach a place of absolute dependence on God.

It is not about being independent from everything but to be fully dependent on Jesus. As this inmate and I finished sharing, he let me know he would send me a letter. He wrote to me, and he said he got to a place where he called out to God, Who he didn't believe in earlier, and he asked Him for forgiveness and mercy. That was almost five years ago. For so many years he was blind. The Bible even talks about those who were blind, and now they can see. He truly understands that it is a gift he received from the Lord. God freely gives when a person desires to see the truth. The inmate stated he has now found the hope to sustain him on the inside of his heart and the walls that surround him.

When he wrote this letter to our church he said he is going back for 20 more years for crimes he admitted to and reminded us that he knows God is love, and He is faithful even when he hasn't been. The hardest thing he has ever done in his life was to surrender to God, but God has prepared him for what is ahead and given him the strength to walk faithfully every day on the inside of the prison walls. Maybe his letter can give us a perspective of thanksgiving to God for continuing to carry the message of hope in a very hopeless world.

I'm closing this chapter with a summary of a letter given through the Commonwealth of Virginia Office of the Capital Defender. The writer's name was Samuel. He shot a total of 5 people, killing 3 of them. I know he has asked God for forgiveness, just as Paul the Apostle asked God for forgiveness for the Christians he helped murder. Samuel explains that it was the love and support of people that set him free, but we know that ultimately it is God who has set him free. He says a true meaning of a friend is a person who is there for someone who has committed a crime like the one he had committed. He says he trusts and prays that all is well with me. He understands God's grace and mercy, maybe more so than many of us ever will. A recent letter he sent ended with John 14:27 (NASB) "Peace I leave with you, my peace I give to you; not as the world gives do I give to you." When I read other parts of the letter it brings tears to my eyes, knowing he is just waiting to be with the Lord. Aren't we all? And God knows that He can forgive all sins. Samuel understands the gift of God's Son, Jesus Christ, Who came to serve and give His life as a ransom for many.

Maybe as you read this there is a desire in your heart to help with jail or prison ministries. In these lonely places it is true that "the harvest is plentiful, but the workers are few" Matthew 9:37b (NIV).

That Day

Everyone remembers "That Day." You may even remember where exactly you were the moment you heard the news. At a pretty large private investment group headquartered in New York City, one of their lead brokerage dealers left and stormed out, not really caring what happened after he left. He could not possibly know what was in his future or the future of his coworkers. Words can be harmful. This was the day that the World Trade Center was hit by two airplanes, and this is how one man's story goes. That September, people were being let go from a very large investment firm due to layoffs. This one individual worked with some co-workers and was very disappointed about the company downsizing. Another individual within that company, Dillon, left and headed to the Outer Banks, North Carolina. Dillon's family was also getting ready for their youngest child to start school.

He may not have his job in New York today, but God saved his life.

Think about if you were the person who stormed out of your office right before the September 11th attack happened, mad at everyone to the point where you didn't really care whether they lived or died. This was a day that no one would forget. Some people cannot move on in their personal lives because of the words they have said to others because of gossip or misunderstanding. Jesus forgave us all when He went to the cross, including all the hurtful things we have said to others and what people have done or said to us.

How many of us are willing to pack up everything and move to a place if the Lord puts it on our heart to move there? What does totally surrendering your life mean? Those in the military do not have a choice when they receive orders to leave. When we leave it all behind for God's glory, we are walking by faith. In life, God allows us to lose things and move us where He needs us, even if it is for a season. This man worked in the World Trade Center and lost his job at the beginning of September. He remembered cleaning out his office and leaving on September 10th. The next day, on September 11th, he would find out from a phone call and television that the office where he once worked was no longer there. I'm sure he thought, "What do you mean, my office is no longer there? I worked in one of the largest buildings in New York City." Imagine being told, "We're sorry to inform you that all the people on the 80th floor of your old company are now deceased." Take time to think about this for a moment. Some still have questions of why. People on many other floors didn't make it that day, yet others above that floor somehow escaped. Maybe you're reading this book and you were there that horrific day. Now at this very moment you think to yourself and hopefully you know that God has a plan in all of this.

Each of you has a story to tell. More importantly, it is the story of how God can rescue those from a falling, burning building. Some may never understand the emotional turmoil that many went through that day, yet others experience emotional trauma on a regular basis. Whether it is a son addicted to drugs, a person losing their job, or a person living through a near-death experience, all these things take place so that God can be glorified in a person's testimony of His providential care. So many people's prayers center on their own needs, but there are many people who need the encouragement of knowing there are people praying for them and people do care.

Isn't it ironic when people ask for prayer or ask to pray for someone, but the answer is no? It could stem from a factor of pride or shame, but it seems to me that we all need prayer. Would you be willing to step out and ask someone how you could be praying for them?

An excerpt from my own journal:
August 2001:

> What does is look like to share the Gospel? To share Christ's love to the lost because God's heart is for everyone including the wandering outcast. When we are sharing the overflow of God's goodness, it is Him working in our lives. And I

pray that He would give me patience while I am discovering life. I pray for my wife, family to be, and that all of them will accept Christ. The more we are blessed in our life, the more we are called to witness about the Lord's blessings. Whoever loves discipline, loves knowledge. The only thing that counts is faith expressing itself through love. If you are running a race and someone cuts in on you and kept you from finishing, it's similar to that of someone disobeying the truth and leading you astray on the race path to the wrong finish line. Remember a little yeast works through a whole batch of dough. If someone is condemning you, hurting you, throwing you into confusion, giving you ultimatums, or pressuring you with expectations, allow God to deal with the situation and the person. In the meantime, just pray for them and love them. Live life by the Spirit and pray for those who live in spiritual blindness to have their eyes opened. Keep living in the Spirit. Every time we make choices it is in God's hands, but no man knows whether love or hate awaits him. We have all taken oaths and whether good or bad, we make sacrifice, but the Lord knows the heart and eternity of all. My prayer is that we live among those whose hope is in the Lord. For the living, know that we will die, and the memory of the dead is slowly forgotten. When we worship, remember worship is a lifestyle. It reminds us who

God is. God loves our worship; it's a part of being
and having an intimate relationship with God. If
you live, live for Christ!

Someone once asked, "Is never sinning again possible?" The
short, easy answer is no. It is like someone playing golf and asking
if a score of 18 is possible? Yes, but unless God gives you this
supernatural ability it's not going to happen. Now I'm not talking
about being forgiven of your sins. This is definitely possible by
the grace of God given to us through Jesus Christ, and we simply
need to accept it! This is more in reference to our old sin nature.
Only one is sinless, and His name is Jesus. He is fully God and
fully man, yet did not sin. I do, however, believe we can sin less
by His grace. Romans chapter 6 is a great part of the Word to
read if you are looking for more clarity on this topic. It really
starts with just listening to the Lord. Sometimes it's essential to
stop and listen. The remarkable thing is that God is waiting for
us to be open to His voice and leading. When we call out to the
Lord, he does not put us on hold. If we desire to talk with God,
have the desire to listen for His voice. You can ask the Lord about
anything, but it is okay if the answer is no. Sometimes the answer
is wait. Other times God may not give you what you ask for, but
He will give you what you need. Traveling over the years along
"life's highway" we need God's Word for a road map. God gives
us great directions and finding the way is much easier if you're
willing to open the map and follow it. God's Word helps us stay
on the right road so that we do not get lost. Romans chapter 1
can put you on the straight and narrow road. Sometimes at the
beginning of your journey you feel like you're ready to go, then

towards the end of the journey, you realize how tired you are, but God gives us the strength to finish the race. The miles in between are some of the toughest. Oftentimes, people pray. This prevents them from getting weary or taking the wrong road. When you think of the church in Philippi (Philippians 4:19-20), God will meet all of our needs.

Maybe you're the type of person that asked, "Where are you God? I don't see you! I don't hear you! I'm having a tough time even understanding, much less following you." When you have difficulty hearing the Lord's voice, ask God to open your ears and learn to be still. This is quite challenging in the world we live in today where there are so many distractions, and we get caught up in all the noise. When we listen, however, the Lord will speak to our hearts, and He will give us the desire to obey those instructions even if we have a rough time keeping on the right course. It's great that we can ask God to help us. Hopefully, just reading this will give you a reminder to thank God for giving you gifts and talents. You have a specific purpose in life, so you can thank God for giving you His special task to do each day to bring Him glory. Desire even your work to bring glory to our God. If you have a job to do, do it as if you were doing it for the Lord. Consequently, you will know that the job you're doing is pleasing, and you can be joyful inside. Know that God sees each moment of your day, and He is pleased with you. He loves you and continually desires us to bring praise to Him. Think about Colossians 3:17a (NASB) "Whatever you do, do all in the name of the Lord Jesus."

Give thanks to God. It's so important to remember to say thank you to others. People get so caught up, going from here to there, that they don't even take moments to say thanks. Maybe at this moment you could pause and give thanks to the Lord. Tell Him you love Him; you desire more of Him; and thank Him for all the blessings He has given you, even the seemingly trivial things like clothes and a bed to sleep in at night. Thank God for physical blessings: you have eyes to see the beauty of His creation; you have ears to hear even the birds sing. Thank God for His spiritual blessings like His love for you, forgiveness, understanding, and guidance. Thank God for the people He has put in your life and has used to encourage you. Thank God for every single thing He is giving you.

Many people have lots of questions today about God and Who He is and that's okay. Questions are great, because they help us clarify things. When a person asks what do you mean, they're asking for clarification. This gives you a chance to explain. When we ask God questions, we go to His Word to find the answers. We can find out more about God, and we will also find out how much God loves us. God teaches us in His Word how to react in certain situations, and He also allows us to know the meaning of true friendship, even if we don't have all the answers. So often we live in a society of pretenders (by going through the motions in ministry) instead of contenders (people contending for the faith and willing to fight the good fight, being thankful that God blesses them by being a part of His ministry). The Bible reminds us that God sees us the way we are on the inside. He sees the incredible love of His Son in you. Yes, even if you've made horrible mistakes in your past, He still sees the person He loves and created. God does not want us to turn church into a show. He desires us to show people Christ.

Don't worry

Don't worry about others; let God fix you first. People wonder why things keep going wrong, but when you ask for directions from the devil you can be sure you're going to be lost.

If you don't kill the pride, the pride will kill you.

When talking to a good friend who has been touring with famous performers, he said being on the road is not a cup of tea by any means. After watching a song by Jimmy Needham titled "Clear the Stage," I sent a text message to a professional big wave surfer and shared with him about how extremely fragile life is. We had the discussion about radical stewardship. When we avoid our own logic, it opens an opportunity for us to think upon God's Word, and His Word does not return void (Isaiah 55:11, KJV).

Think about the word *hashena* for a minute. At one point we had thought of changing our ministry to this name. The meaning of this word is "The nature of a person's heart that is doing what is honorable and right in the sight of the Lord." Only God knows the heart. We are not to judge outside the body of Christ, and when we look within, remember that we know God's people by their fruit. Are we willing to give up our home? Our car? Our possessions? All for God's glory? Not many of us would want to. Understandably. We all have weaknesses, and we are not to look down on those who are comfortable where they are. What many people are learning today is that God uses us when we are out of our comfort zone. The Christian life of faith has never been about being comfortable, unless we are comfortable in Christ.

CHAPTER TWELVE

Destination Anywhere

Obedience is what some would call compliance with an order, request, or submission to another's authority. In this case, much like in the military, believing what the commander has asked of you. For me it is being certain of what God says is true. Here is the story of a guy in college:

He asked others and myself about how he could be delivered from having a same sex attraction and how then SSA progressed to him choosing the lifestyle of being homosexual. In response, someone in the group asked him how can homosexuality be genetic if you cannot continue to procreate and pass the trait or gene on, because it would then cease to exist. It would not evolve according to evolutionist theory, unless it's recessive. Better yet, do we place our belief on genetics or on the infallible Word of God? Where do we stand on these issues? Why do we reject Christ is a better question? When we turn away from Christ, it is sin and our desire to fill our lives with what we think is going to satisfy us. Some people think Christians are judgmental and unkind. The truth is, we all can be this way, whether we are Christians or not. Maybe it is Satan. He has just blinded us, because he doesn't want people hearing God's Word or about Jesus. If we don't have Jesus, then we can't have conviction. Maybe our society, culture, and world, just needs to listen. Hebrews 2:1 (NLT) says: "So we must listen very carefully to the truth we have heard, or we may drift away from it." Today, more than ever, we need to hear the truth, which is that God loves us and wants us to believe he has healed us when we give our life to Him.

What you are about to read next from the account of friends, family, and their personal stories is a narrative of individuals being delivered.

God was going to move in a huge way once we got on the road. We stopped at a three-way fork in the road by the Northwest River Park sign. It was dark, and I did not have peace about Mickey or Oscar getting out of the van. But, as most surfers can tell you, they like to represent the brands that sponsor them by tagging signs with stickers. Early in the morning, before sunrise, Mickey did not have peace, and as Oscar got ready to put a sticker on a sign, the Lord moved in my spirit to tell him, "Get out of the road!" less than five seconds later a near head-on collision happened as both vehicles skidded past one another right on that road where Oscar was standing. If it were not for God's protection, he may have gotten hit right at that moment. It really woke up Oscar and Mickey. As we were driving along down to North Carolina, Oscar said he wanted to accept Jesus Christ into his heart.

The events leading up to this point started with me just hanging out with a group of young guys I surfed with and for years, I just spent time with them. The amazing thing was, that night, Oscar accepted Christ into his heart around 8 p.m. on the back roads, and then Mickey prayed the same prayer about 10 minutes later. It was such a blessing and honor to be with them and witness all this, so we headed over to a little fast food place on the side of the road and had a little mini celebration. We got back on the road, and after reading the Gospels of John, Mark Chapter 1, and Matthew chapter 5, we were crossing over the Wright Brothers Memorial Bridge, they both wanted to be filled with the Holy Spirit. I reassured them that they had the Father, the Son, and the Holy Spirit when they gave their life to Jesus Christ, explaining that we can always ask to be filled with the Spirit. It's a blessing to know that when the spirit is leading you, you can trust in him knowing that God hears and answers our prayers. Amen.

Freedom from demon possession on Halloween night

One Halloween afternoon, a dear friend of mine, Tom, and I decided to meet up and have a few people over to a new church we were attending. He had been unintentionally fasting and another individual was as well. We did not know at the time, but there is a Bible verse that indicates that these demons are only cast out by prayer and fasting, see Matthew 17:21. In some translations it is omitted, but we stumbled across it after this event. So here is the rest of the story from Tom's account:

After the pizza arrived at the church fellowship hall we were all hanging out. I introduced myself to a new young man who came with another young lady. She said, "He is having some problems." They believed this individual was under some type of oppression – some type of evil, specifically a demon. I felt the same after introducing myself to him when he did not respond. I then asked another question to break the ice, "What are you listening to?" The screen on his phone displayed the word Lucifer. This was not only strange, but certainly unexplainable unless, of course, it was his screen saver. When he finally said something to me, it sounded like "for I am many". Then he continued to speak.

It sounded like he said, "You asked my name, and I am Legion." In the Bible it says the demon-possessed man stated his name was Legion. Which reminded me of Mark 5:9 (NIV), "Then Jesus asked him, 'What is your name?' 'My name is Legion,' he replied, 'for we are many.'"

At this point, I became very uncomfortable. I called a friend that was a pastor at another church in the area, and his suggestion was to cast the demon out. My logical mindset was to call the local authorities because of the situation that was unfolding. Most people, in any situation like this, where another person is threatening someone's life, would call the police. In this case, the only backup we had was Jesus. If you are like some people who are surrendered to the Lord, life doesn't really matter much. Ultimately, we depend on Him and not our logic. Once I looked back, he had the same young lady who brought him to the gathering in a headlock and was choking her. The next thing I knew, Tom and I were trying to detain this young man and praying for the demons to be cast out in the name of Jesus. Tom specifically prayed to cast them into the rabbits because there were no pigs anywhere near us, but earlier that night he did see a few rabbits outside in the church lawn. Tom knew that during Jesus ministry, He had cast demons into a herd of pigs. The demons pleaded with Him to have more time on Earth, they didn't want to be sent directly to Hell, which is their destination. Meanwhile, freeing this young lady from bodily harm was our main concern. Once she was freed, we then tried to calm him and asked him to have a seat. Thank God, the police arrived at that moment. Thinking to myself, "Wow, are we really in a church building?" I have seen and witnessed some crazy things in my life, but this was certainly one that made the top of the list. The officers came in, and to my surprise, I knew one of the officers.

He said, "Hi, Troy how are you doing?"

I replied, "I have had better days. This young man was just choking this young lady."

The officer then asked if she would like to press charges. To everyone's surprise her response was no. She asked if she could privately speak to the guy she came with and me. Once alone, she asked, "Would you like to be free from any other demonic attacks, have eternal life, and be saved and rescued?" He said, "Yes."

This man then prayed with everyone there, even in front of the officers. This was a testimony to all of us, even the police officers who responded. Then they asked how this man was going to get home. Never in a million years would I have thought we would be taking him home in Tom's car. The event came to an abrupt ending, and five individuals got into Tom's vehicle. We proceeded to drop this new Christian off at his home. I remember quite clearly asking him, "Do you even remember what happened?"

He said, "All I remember is praying to accept Jesus Christ into my heart, and I don't feel darkness around me any longer."

Thank God! After he got out of the car we all could not believe what had taken place. Tom then dropped me back off at the church building, and I drove home. Getting back to those rabbits, you might be wondering what happened to them. I got a strange call around one o'clock in the morning from Tom, who saw a rabbit in his yard when he returned home that night. He was very apprehensive to get out of his vehicle. The next day, when he woke up, there was a dead rabbit next to his doorstep, similar to the pigs in the Bible who went off to drown.

What are the chances of all this taking place? I asked Tom if he was certain that it was a rabbit and not a squirrel. But he said something to the effect of he knows what rabbits look like.

There was another very similar experience that took place on Oahu with a family that lived near the Punchbowl Cemetery. One day this young man named Aaron asked me to come over to his home to pray over his apartment and for his family to stop being oppressed by the demonic presence they felt. When I asked him to describe the situation, he informed me that his little infant would wake up screaming at night, and they noticed scratches on the child. His wife thought her husband was doing all of this. To prove it, they both stayed up one night together, and it happened again. At that point, they both knew that it was something they could not explain. I visited with Aaron, and the place they lived in had a very dark presence about it. When we finally entered the apartment, the rooms were very cold and felt empty – an unusual situation to say the least. The next thing you know, Aaron and I just started to pray for freedom from the oppressive spirits traumatizing his family. We prayed until we felt led to stop. The wonderful news came about a month later, when Aaron informed me that the screaming had stopped and there were no more scratches on his child anymore. Today, by the grace of God, there is freedom from the demons that had been attacking that family in Hawaii.

Freedom from the addiction of same sex attraction and homosexuality

When you think about transformation, please understand that our daily lives are either devoted to God or to this world.

Over the past twenty years, looking at my collection of stories, I realized that they provide God's story through me to reach those that may have never heard the Gospel. When reading Scripture, we may not understand the Bible. The Bible is the inspired Word of God, and God at any moment, can use His Word to speak to you. At any place. Anywhere. Anytime.

What the Lord has taught me over the years is to pray for His wisdom, just as it says in James 1:5 "If any of you lacks wisdom, let him ask God, who gives generously to all without reproach, and it will be given him" (ESV).

God gave us all a mission to complete with Him by our side, not without Him. A soldier without a plan is a soldier planning to fail on the mission. If a person is a Christian they are a soldier in the Lord's army, and part of the body of Christ. God desires us to love Him and have a personal relationship with Him. Through that relationship, understanding and growth in His Word eventually take place.

God's Word is clear that we are all called to do the work of an evangelist. Maybe you're reading right now and wondering, "What does God have planned for the life He has given me?" Maybe you do not believe you are called to do this work. Please pause for a moment. Begin by praying and asking God to speak to your heart: God, please reveal Your will for my life. Speak to my heart and have me understand how You would use me to further Your kingdom.

Maybe you are already in the position of serving or helping in a ministry. Maybe your prayer may be something like this: Lord, send people to help serve, and Lord, help me to trust that You have the right people, and You will send them at just the right time. In fact, God did this for my friend I mentioned earlier who struggled with SSA and homosexuality. His desire was always to be free from sexual addiction, and after fellow believers prayed for him, he said he desired God more than he desired intimacy with anyone else. He ultimately learned the longing he had could only be fulfilled with the intimacy of a loving, caring, gracious God. Today he is choosing to live free from this addiction. Praise God!

While waiting on God, we can start by reading His Word and praying. Daily reading of God's Word maximizes the potential for God's revelation in your personal life. He knows the desires and concerns of your heart that may be present at this very moment or at any moment where you read His word.

Let's change gears for a moment

Hopefully, the reading, praying, and living out the Gospel is a part of your daily schedule, but please do not become legalistic about it. Legalism is a heart condition and is just going through the motions. Ultimately God desires us to have an authentic hunger for Him, leading to our being rescued from ourselves. When things become so regimented, we can lose focus on the grace of God. We are reminded of this in Matthew 28:19a (NIV) "make disciples of all nations". God's Word also directs us to be "fishers of men." When was the last time that you went fishing? When we live out our life to the fullest in Christ, His message speaks through us! God is spreading the Gospel message through us wherever and whenever we glorify Him. God is our greatest source of encouragement, guidance, and unfailing love.

God doesn't just give us a new beginning at the start of a new year. He gives us a new and fresh start every day. Yesterday is in the past, and we cannot change it. There is a saying: enjoy the present. The present is a gift. We can have hope for the future, but our hope comes from Jesus and tomorrow is not promised, so go and enjoy the day that God has given you. God says in 1 John 1:9 "If we confess our sins, He is faithful and just and will forgive us our sins and purify us from all unrighteousness" (NIV). Notice the emphasis on the word "will," not "if" or "but". God will forgive us our sins when we ask Him for forgiveness. Remember, you are not alone. God's Word says in Romans 3:23, "For all have sinned and fall short of the glory of God" (ESV). However, take great comfort, God's Word also says He is just, merciful, gracious, and forgiving. He is a loving God. The kindness of God draws people to repentance. Through God's Son, Jesus Christ, we can all be forgiven, justified, and purified in Him.

When you think of Romans chapter 6 verses 1- 14 you cannot help but think of the reason we believe. When we give and surrender our lives to Christ, He gives us the strength to fight for the true freedom in Him. Many people in the church today are struggling with all types of sin – everything from alcohol, anger, pornography, and drugs, just to mention some. When you think of the enemy, he wants to keep us trapped. The way a person is set free is in Jesus Christ. When we surrender our life to Him He says we are dead to sin. He sets us free from the bondage of sin. We are justified in Him. This means we are declared not guilty. This is what justification is. When we think of the term sanctification, we are then growing more like Christ. Molded and shaped into His image for God's glory so that others may see Him in us. As believers we are growing in grace towards God because of His mercy and saving grace. Furthermore, because of this we are unified with Christ, we are trusting in God for sanctification and destined to win because of Christ's victory over death. When a person is struggling in sin, my prayer is that they know Christ has renewed them, restored them, and redeemed them. When we look at verse 3 and verse 14 in the 6th chapter, we see that we are alive to God and dead to sin. The Holy Spirit in us gives us strength and by His grace brings us victory in Jesus.

I have heard it once said: leave your struggles behind. It is like a person trusting in Jesus and beginning their journey through life with Him. Jesus then invites them on a plane ride and wonderful vacation, and He says, "The destination is paradise." Jesus is our pilot in life. We must let go of trying to direct the plane to where we want it to go. The best thing about taking this journey with Jesus is that He asks us to leave our baggage behind. No luggage (anxiety, pain, struggles, or depression) is necessary when we understand the freedom we have in Christ and it gives us the ability for God to use us in amazing ways.

The wonderful thing about trusting in God is that He gives us the Holy Spirit to lead us, comfort us, and guide us along the path of life. Please remember: sometimes along the journey it may be challenging and difficult at times. Also, bear in mind the goal is to focus on Jesus when it becomes a challenge and it seems hard to keep going. The enemy is very good at reminding us of our past failures, hardships, and shortcomings. This is when we can be reminded that God's Word states that our old past has been wiped away and that we have become "a new creation" (2 Corinthians 5:17). We are new! We have a new life and a new beginning. It starts with our acknowledgement and faith in Jesus Christ.

My own apprehension

I remember long ago saying I would never do something. I would never do this, or I would never do that. I've learned not to use the word never. If you tell God you're never going to do something, it's almost like a guarantee you are probably going to end up doing it. I remember reading Romans 10:14 thinking my family, friends and others would hear, but "how shall they believe in Him of who they have not heard?" God put this action on my heart long ago, but I was too prideful, stubborn, and thought I was good at running away from God. Believe me: God can outrun you. When you get tired of running, He is there to embrace you in His loving arms. It was at that moment when I knew God was asking me to share the Gospel of His grace with those who are lost. Most of us have heard the joyful saying, "Jesus Saves." Jesus saves us, rescues us, shapes us, and unconditionally loves us till the day that we are with Him in Heaven.

The story of Jackson

Jackson came into my life in such a strange way. He would say, much like myself, that the name that matters most in this story is Jesus Christ. He comes into our lives at the most unexpected moments we can imagine, when we are ready to give up on life. He can give us clarity in any situation, including when we are under the influence of alcohol or drugs.

Jackson's story is about God intervening when we are out of control. This young man got on his bike and decided he was going to ride across the country. He was out of control in a major way. When he was going through the mountains of Colorado, he got a flat tire, and after changing the bike tire, he was about to ride down the other side of the mountain. He was thankful for the beauty God created, and as he went to apply the brake, he realized a key component of braking, connecting the brake cable to the brake pads, had been skipped in his haste to change the tire. At this point he thought, "God, I'm going really fast. I'm out of control and desperately need you to intervene in this situation." Being totally out of control and listening to this account from Jackson always brings a smile to my face and a little laughter, because he said he was looking for one of those run-off ramps for semi-trucks. He said he didn't see anything of that sort in sight. All he knew was that he was going at a very high rate of speed and prayed. At that moment, he noticed that there was a patch of sand on the side of the road, which spared him from getting in a horrible accident on a very steep mountain. The funny thing was when he stopped, his tire was flat again. He didn't have any inner tubes left or a way to fix it, but then he thought, "Maybe God provided this sand for more than one reason." Not only to stop, but to fill the inside of the tube to give it stability on the way down. Once he got to the bottom he stopped in at a gas station and fixed the tire there. After hearing this story, I can't help but think how God gives us exactly what we need at the exact moment along our journey through life. And he uses some of the things to develop our faith. For me, personally, I have seen God's hand provide for the desires of people's hearts. For others, they are running on flat tires in their spiritual life. If that's you, use the "sand" He provides to keep you going.

The next story is also Jackson's, which he admits is more peculiar than the last. One day he thought to himself, "How amazing would it be to see a squirrel close up?" He spent that night sleeping outdoors, and the next morning he remembered feeling something inside his sleeping bag. He felt something climbing up the inside of his jeans, and he was very nervous and fearful. After a few moments of anticipation, a squirrel popped out in front of his face. How funny! Even with something as small as seeing a squirrel up close, God did grant him the desire of his heart.

So often we think God isn't hearing our prayers, but it may just be a season of waiting patiently. This does not mean God did not hear us. It does mean that we have a prerequisite to trust that His timing is perfect. Waiting for His timing develops patience, perseverance, and character. God will give you one of four answers to prayer: yes, no, wait, or maybe. In this case, maybe means do it yourself. I use that phrase cautiously and very often! When we take things into our own hands, we tend to make things worse. In contrast, if God has already given you the ability and provided the open door, it is up to you to walk through it. Salvation is one of those open doors. Everyone who opens their heart and believes in Christ can walk through it.

The answers God gives you also depends on your true desires. Are you asking for money or comfort? Are you asking for a house or for you to make a place a home? Are you asking for a bed or for rest? Are you asking Him for a partner or for true love? Jesus is not a genie per say, so sometimes material requests get a "wait" answer while He is preparing you or the thing. Your character must be developed first, and He wants you to delight in His gifts. Sure, you can buy a peace sign, but you can't buy peace in your heart. Salvation is the first gift you receive simply by asking Him into your heart.

Looking at all the adventures addressed in this book hopefully gives you a glimpse into what it looks like to develop a relationship with Jesus. Of course, they all are nothing in comparison to what we can look forward to as that relationship matures in intimacy. A principle that is dear to me is having a grateful heart, even when going through difficult circumstances. A grateful heart also paves the way for reconciliation. The ministry of reconciliation is talked about in 2 Corinthians 5:17. It says, "Therefore, if anyone is in Christ, he is a new creation. The old has passed away; behold, the new has come" (ESV).

2 Corinthians 5:11-21 (ESV) says:

> Therefore, knowing the fear of the Lord, we persuade others. But what we are is known to God, and I hope it is known also to your conscience. We are not commending ourselves to you again but giving you cause to boast about us, so that you may be able to answer those who boast about outward appearance and not about what is in the heart. For if we are beside ourselves, it is for God; if we are in our right mind, it is for you. For the love of Christ controls us, because we have concluded this: that one has died for all, therefore all have died; and he died for all, that those who live might no longer live for themselves but for him who for their sake died and was raised. From now on, therefore, we regard no one according to the flesh. Even though we once regarded Christ according to the flesh, we regard him thus no

longer. Therefore, if anyone is in Christ, he is a new creation. The old has passed away; behold, the new has come. All this is from God, who through Christ reconciled us to himself and gave us the ministry of reconciliation; that is, in Christ God was reconciling the world to himself, not counting their trespasses against them, and entrusting to us the message of reconciliation. Therefore, we are ambassadors for Christ, God making his appeal through us. We implore you on behalf of Christ, be reconciled to God. For our sake he made him to be sin who knew no sin, so that in him we might become the righteousness of God.

When thinking of this verse in context, it reminds me that all of us have a past and a choice. We can look back, or we can look forward. God, at this moment, may be asking you to be reconciled to Him. He has given us the ministry of reconciliation that is in Christ. He does not hold our sin against us, but He is a loving God we can trust. The reason for sharing this verse here is so that we can all share in the righteousness of God. Therefore, Jesus came to die for our sins and was raised from the dead. He reconciled us to Himself through Jesus' sacrifice on the cross. He is a God who is alive and one of my prayers is that the love of Christ would lead each of us as we go on our journey of faith.

CHAPTER THIRTEEN

The FSS and The Sewer

Costa Rica will always have a special place in my heart. It means "the rich coast." When I was there the second time, I found true riches in a very profound way. I knew that my riches were in the Kingdom of God, and discovering the beautiful landscape while taking time to reflect made me realize that only God can fill an empty heart. When you take a trip here to surf there are so many remote places that are uncrowded and peaceful. One day after driving with some friends down to the beach and seeing empty line-ups (which means no one is in the water) we paddled out. I came to the realization of just how small I was in the grand scheme of things. I reminisced about my past and was thankful God brought me to a place like this to understand that God not only had a plan for my life, but that one day this story may help someone come to the same conclusion. Every time I've traveled there, the surf seems to be pretty consistent, but I came to the understanding that God's love for me is more consistent than any wave on Earth, even better than a wave ranch. As much as I enjoyed surfing, I enjoyed knowing that God's love for me was always there. Often, people can reject God's love or try to replace it with things or addictions. Some of my closest friends have told me, "Man, I'm addicted to surfing. I blow off weddings, and I've even blown off a few funerals. I just want to surf." I can relate to this, being a surfer. I've never regretted being at a funeral or a wedding where close friends have given their lives to one another.

When you have a heart for a certain people or place, God oftentimes shows you that you have free will to take the opportunity to go. Maybe at this moment you are thinking of a place where you would like to go, and when you share God's amazing love He opens doors. Are we willing to walk through them?

On this particular trip to Costa Rica, we went to a river mouth close to Tamarindo called Playa Langosta. The difficulty level is probably for experienced surfers, especially when there is a large, straight west swell coming in, but when the surf is good, the rights can be amazing. Just make sure the tide doesn't get too low while you are surfing on the outside break, because you will be fixing your board like I had to. I somehow managed to slam into rock on the way in and realized, "Man there are rocks here after all!" While I was there I wrote in my journal that the sun was so hot on my green board, which I had just finished fixing, that it melted the wax off faster than I could put it on. The sun is pretty intense there. On January 7th I journaled that I made a necklace for my wife-to-be. Then I surfed that same river mouth that morning. I remember swimming across the river mouth and I lost my sandal, which was unfortunate, especially when I got out of the water at about 11, and the sand was really hot. The good thing was someone found my sandal for me and gave it back! Once I returned to where I was staying, I caught an iguana to see if I could. Be careful: these things bite! Some people learn this the hard way. Later that day I was reading a Bible that I took along with me on this trip and recall listening to the monkeys making a bunch of noise. One of the reasons I enjoyed being in this place was because I left all the noise and distractions of where I was living and desperately needed a break. When I returned home, the air temperature was six degrees and I said to myself, "I cannot live here! I have to move South and to warm weather if it's God's will." Sure enough, as these words are being typed, my family and I live in Hawaii. It isn't necessarily south, meaning Florida. It's a warm place, and God had a better plan.

I realized I might have some symptoms of "Frantic Soul Syndrome." If you have any of the following symptoms, you may have FSS:

1. You don't think you have it, but you think everyone else has it
2. Always in a hurry and lack of patience with others around you
3. Clutter all around you
4. Buying a lot of things for your home to add to the clutter and mess you already live in
5. Staying busy and avoiding real relationships

The great news is that there is a solution to this so-called FSS. You could pick the longest line occasionally when you are checking out at a store. Better yet, let someone go in front of you. If clutter is your struggle, you can clean up the mess around you and help others by asking them to put things back where they belong. Ultimately, get rid of the things you don't need. There really is some truth behind the whole minimalist movement, because things can take up space and managing them takes up time. While I was in Costa Rica, I pondered some of this. One thing is for certain, when I seem to get too busy with stuff, it's time to seek solitude. Here are a few suggestions that may help. Have a quiet time reading God's Word and talking with Him in the morning. Purge distractions by turning off your phone, computer, and your tv. At the end of this journal entry on this trip I started to focus on all the things I could be thankful for and that God has provided. Now looking back at that trip, it is clear that God provided great surfing, put people in my life who were willing to confront me when I made mistakes and provided us a place to stay, a car to use, and we did nothing to acquire any of these things. We allowed God to move in our lives and trust Him.

The Sewer

Some of us are living life in a sewer, and others are just trying to get over the dirty canal of our past. We are in the Lord's hands. We humans think we have control, but God is in control. All we can do is listen, trust, and obey God. Being obedient can be one of the hardest things to do, especially if you pray that intense prayer for patience and God says wait on Him. God's timing is perfect, and He knew when I would start writing this book. What is our hope in life? Sometimes we desire our will so badly, we get so sidetracked, or we get so unfocused, that it is hard to see God working in our lives. We can all get sidetracked in life even when following instructions. This is much like the people who followed Jesus wherever He went, but in the end, they had a hope in the final and wonderful conclusion of the story that is His wonderful redemption!

To make things clear, God delivered me from myself. It does not matter how you get there, if you finish with God by your side. Be willing to ask God daily for a desire to do His will, and rest assured that He will complete the good work He has started in you. Please ponder the Word daily for a moment. Everyday a person must die to their flesh to do the Father's will (Romans 8:13).

Consider this story of a young child, now a man, who looks back into his past. He sees and recalls a life of disaster and brokenness. If it had not been for a man coming along to rescue him, he would have never seen the love he was looking for or the comfort he needed. On this day, I remember picking up a rock a lot larger than I thought it was, thinking how awesome it would be to throw this rock in the water to just see a big splash. There is usually a big splash when you throw a rock in the water, especially if you do not remember to let go. I followed that rock right into the lake, and if it wasn't for my cousin, I would have gone right down into the culvert, through the spillway, and drowned. Our hope is in Christ. This was not the first time I would take a fall into water nor would it be the last.

As a young kid, I always thought I could jump anything on my bike, including the canal down the street from my childhood home. There I was, pedaling down the side of the hill, with a big crowd watching. Looking back, five of your childhood friends probably does not constitute a "big crowd," but when you are young, anything over three is a crowd. At this point, I had every intention of jumping over and clearing the canal. Midway through flight, I realized that my momentum and imagination would not carry me to the other side. Still I was holding onto the handlebars in hopes that my bike could float. It didn't. My bike and I sunk to the bottom. It was nasty on the bottom and murky, so I left my bike in there at the bottom and came home muddy and wet.

When I showed up at the door, my dad asked how I ended up soaking wet and muddy.

I was forced to explain the stunt that ended in failure and in return said I needed to go back and get my bike. "There is no excuse to leave it there on the bottom," he said. Did my dad realize how gross this canal was? Fishing it out would be a whole new adventure. A friend came with me, and we did fish it out with a very large hook and strong line. We threw the hook repeatedly until we snagged it and slowly pulled it up off the bottom. This illustrates what God can do in our lives if we allow Him. He comes and picks us up when we have been defeated or have failed. Whether we are trying to jump over water on our bike and fall in or navigate through a troubled relationship, God can step in at any moment and pull us up from the bottom of despair and clean us up from the muddy mess we made. God is gracious, loving, and merciful. Our Father in Heaven knows just how nasty and gross some of the things in our past are, and He is faithful to forgive when we ask Him. God can carry anyone to the other side if we are willing to allow Him.

Growing up where I did offered many opportunities for me to understand God's grace. It was great to have neighbors who would share their life experiences and advice with a young kid like me. I have always been very inquisitive and have asked a lot of questions. This is how people learn. The day I was invited over to Chris & Cynthia's house is the day I learned about this man named Jesus. Growing up, my parents would take me to church, but I knew more about methodology than about my relationship with Christ. Their daughter, Ann, told me she went to a Messianic Jewish church. Like any twelve-year old would ask, "Oh you're

Jewish?" She said, "We believe that Jesus Christ is the Messiah, and we celebrate Jewish culture." I wasn't sure what that meant, but replied, "Sounds good to me, I'll let my Dad know." With this all being said, my neighbors invited me along to visit this small congregation of Messianic believers.

This is where I met a man who started to invest in my life and disciple me. He taught me Hebrew phrases, told me what a Bar Mitzvah is, and gave me a book on Reggie White, a great football player. I knew that this man, Chris, cared and desired for me to seek out faith and to discern what that meant for me. He was not pushy and did not have all the answers, but he challenged me to find what faith was on my own. At this point in my life, I was holding onto a lot of my early childhood hurts and pain, but I knew only God could take away the pain. The Holy Spirit leads us in so many ways. He is there even before we give our life to the Lord.

> About that time the disciples came to Jesus and asked, "Who is greatest in the Kingdom of Heaven?" Jesus called a little child to him and put the child among them. Then he said, "I tell you the truth, unless you turn from your sins and become like little children, you will never get into the Kingdom of Heaven. So, anyone who becomes as humble as this little child is the greatest in the Kingdom of Heaven. Matthew 18:1-4(NLT)

I knew a Jewish guy, named Fritz, and he shared the Gospel with another man named Carl. Little did they know at the time that they had the same girlfriend. This night started with Fritz calling the girlfriend, however, neither knew the girlfriend had any other relationships. Carl decided to look at his girlfriend's cell phone, got the number, and then left the house. After getting into the car and calling the number, he then proceeded to ask some questions about his girlfriend, and then asked where he could meet the man on the other end of the phone. Carl met up with Fritz where he then explained to him that instead of sleeping with Fritz's girlfriend, he saw the phone call and wanted to get to the bottom of it. After they talked for a few minutes, Fritz realized that Carl indeed knew his girlfriend, and Carl then told Fritz that he did not sleep with this girl because he was convicted by the Holy Spirit that it would not honor God.

Carl then explained that he would not be seeing her anymore, because he knew that he was lied to, but he thought that it would also be honorable to let Fritz know the truth. Fritz had to ask, "Who would do this? Who would show up to someone's house to tell them the truth about their girlfriend?" Carl explained that he heard Fritz had been dating this person for five years. Fritz said they had dated even longer than that. Carl really felt bad for Fritz. "This whole relationship you have with this person is based on a lie. We can build our lives on a lie, believing someone really truly loves us. But the only person that really loves you, Fritz, is Jesus. The Lord wants you to know the truth, and I know that you believe in God, but Jesus also says, 'believe in me.'" Carl will never know the impact of this night, but his hope was that God leading him there ultimately led Fritz to a relationship with Jesus Christ, instead of a broken relationship with a girl.

When a person loses three children to miscarriages and misses six attempts to purchase a home, it doesn't matter where a person is in their walk, they will have questions. When door after door closes, you start to think, "God why are you allowing us to go through all these disappointments?" However, in the suffering and hardships, you can only have peace in His grace, presence, and hope. When you read Isaiah 40:31a, "Those who hope in the Lord will renew their strength" (NIV). I know for me, I have felt pretty strong over the past year, and I know that can only be God's work in my life. Clearly God is showing me that we were in a season of being comfortable where we didn't want to be. Now we are in a season where we have peace about where we need to be, but it's not comfortable.

God has taught me many lessons over the years, but most of them can be boiled down to these couple of statements that I've learned through life's storms and hardships:

- Addiction is an attempt to fix or fill an emotional impairment or void
- People are coming to the church with brokenness and pain. God speaks to us through His word with compassion, healing, and authority. Please read Matthew 7
- Read God's Word and write out the passages that stand out for you.
- It is not about acting like a Christian. It is about being one. Jesus was the only perfect human.
- Everyone is searching for something. Ultimately what we need is Jesus.
- Idolatry is anything that we worship instead of God.
- Seeking pleasure will not bring fulfillment. It can only come from God.

Our Christian life is like scuba diving, and the Bible is our air. Think about how many people have died scuba diving because they didn't learn from people that knew what they were doing before them, and they did not listen to instructions. They ended up drowning. Learn now so you are not dead in sin later!

Sometimes we don't realize that we're walking in darkness and that we're trapped. A good illustration is you're going into a cave, and you need a light to see. What if your light goes out? Instantly you realize that you're in darkness, and you're hoping that somebody else has a flashlight. Once they turn on the light, the light helps you and others get out of the darkness. The cave that you're stuck in seems like a hopeless situation. However, you would never know that you were walking in darkness unless you knew what a light was. A flashlight lights the pathway, and this is the same way that Jesus lights our path in life, giving us hope in hopeless situations. Hopefully we can see and recognize our way out of sin and darkness is only with Jesus Christ leading the way. He came to set people free so that we were no longer trapped in a place of despair and complete darkness.

1 Peter 1:3-9 (NLT) is a great chapter and below is part of the chapter to help clarify any misconceptions when sharing the hope of eternal life with others:

> All praise to God, the Father of our Lord Jesus Christ. It is by his great mercy that we have been born again, because God raised Jesus Christ from the dead. Now we live with great expectation, and we have a priceless inheritance—an inheritance that is kept in heaven for you, pure and undefiled,

beyond the reach of change and decay. And through your faith, God is protecting you by his power until you receive this salvation, which is ready to be revealed on the last day for all to see. So be truly glad. There is wonderful joy ahead, even though you must endure many trials for a little while. These trials will show that your faith is genuine. It is being tested as fire tests and purifies gold—though your faith is far more precious than mere gold. So, when your faith remains strong through many trials, it will bring you much praise and glory and honor on the day when Jesus Christ is revealed to the entire world. You love him even though you have never seen him. Though you do not see him now, you trust him; and you rejoice with a glorious, inexpressible joy. The reward for trusting him will be the salvation of your souls.

A friend of mine once said nobody wants to hear when they are wrong. Some judge and criticize others without knowing the whole situation. When a person is presented with the truth it can be difficult. It's like a lawyer building or presenting a case, and then when the truth is presented they do not like the fact that they are incorrect. They don't want to accept the indictment. This is much like people when Jesus Christ is presented to them as the Way to be rescued and redeemed. They reject the Truth when they don't accept Him. There is no alternative other than being separated from God. This, then, leads them to remaining in judgment. Our freedom from judgment is the truth of the Gospel.

Jesus, Who rescued us from death and reconciled us to Himself through death on the cross. Redemption is through Jesus Christ, and we await His return to redeem us. Salvation ultimately is through us being reconciled to God through Him. He came to die so that we could live. Death to life! Justified by God's grace.

> "But these are written so that you may believe that Jesus is the Christ, the Son of God, and that by believing you may have life in his name" John 20:31 (ESV).

> "When everything is ready, I will come and get you, so that you will always be with me where I am" John 14:3 (NLT).

My hope for you, as a reader, is that if you do not know Jesus or what it means to have a conversion, that you would make a decision for Christ today. You have a choice: you may ask what this is, you may refuse to hear the voice of God. Jesus will not force you. Hopefully you will open the door to let Him into your heart. Not opening the door means to shut Him out or keep Jesus from coming into your life. To have a meal together with a person is an outward example of love and reconciliation with God and the amazing forgiveness brought to us by His Son Jesus. Will you, today, open the door to your heart and let Jesus in?

> "Look! I stand at the door and knock. If you hear my voice and open the door, I will come in, and we will share a meal together as friends" Revelation 3:20 (NLT).

He sees everything in our lives: the good times and the bad. He is there with us through each step of our lives. This brings delight to my heart knowing at this moment, someone reading this right now, might open their heart to Jesus, and allow Him to give them a new life. When a person accepts Jesus into their heart:

It is the LORD who goes before you. He will be with you; he will not leave you or forsake you. Do not fear or be dismayed Deuteronomy 31:8 (ESV).

-THE END-

EPILOGUE

My prayer and hope are that you will share your story and your faith with those around you. When you share the love of Christ with the lost, it gives them the opportunity to have the same hope you have in a world which is perishing and hopeless.

Remember God has done great and wonderful things in your life. He created you for a purpose, and please remember to share without fear! Be bold for Jesus Christ by sharing the message of redemption which can be found only in Him through His Word.

May His Holy Spirit lead you and guide you.

ABOUT THE AUTHOR

Ezekiel Smith knows it's not about him; it's about Jesus – His love, His forgiveness, His grace. He is an entrepreneur, logistics guru, author, encourager, helps with a non-profit, and a graduate of Virginia Tech. He really lives out his faith. He enjoys surfing, fishing, and living near the ocean with his wife and family.

Passionate, perseverant, fun, thankful, hard to describe, outgoing, and so many other words have been used to describe Ezekiel Smith. This book has hopefully given you some insight into the incomprehensibility of God. We all deserve to have a life that is full of love, God's grace, satisfaction in Christ, and hope. Faith is where it all begins.

Thank you, Jesus, for putting Your loving arms around me when I need it. Lord, You know my heart and give me strength to continue in the life You have blessed me with for Your glory. With Your strength, Christ, and the Holy Spirit gently guiding me, may Your Kingdom Come, and Your will be done.